# Spirit-Empowered Witness

## A Lukan Theology of Preaching

David N. Gambo

© 2022 David N. Gambo

Published 2022 by Langham Academic (Previously Langham Monographs)
*An imprint of Langham Publishing*
www.langhampublishing.org

Langham Publishing and its imprints are a ministry of Langham Partnership

Langham Partnership
PO Box 296, Carlisle, Cumbria, CA3 9WZ, UK
www.langham.org

ISBNs:
978-1-83973-586-8 Print
978-1-83973-628-5 ePub
978-1-83973-630-8 PDF

David N. Gambo has asserted his right under the Copyright, Designs and Patents Act, 1988 to be identified as the Author of this work.

All rights reserved. No part of this publication may be reproduced, stored in a retrieval system or transmitted, in any form or by any means, electronic, mechanical, photocopying, recording or otherwise, without the prior written permission of the publisher or the Copyright Licensing Agency.

Requests to reuse content from Langham Publishing are processed through PLSclear. Please visit www.plsclear.com to complete your request.

Unless otherwise stated, all Scripture translations in this work are the author's own.

Scripture quotations marked (NASB) are taken from the New American Standard Bible®, Copyright © 1960, 1962, 1963, 1968, 1971, 1972, 1973, 1975, 1977, 1995 by The Lockman Foundation. Used by permission.

Scripture quotations marked (NKJV) are taken from the New King James Version (NKJV). Copyright © 1982 by Thomas Nelson, Inc. Used by permission. All rights reserved.

**British Library Cataloguing-in-Publication Data**
A catalogue record for this book is available from the British Library

ISBN: 978-1-83973-586-8

Cover & Book Design: projectluz.com

Langham Partnership actively supports theological dialogue and an author's right to publish but does not necessarily endorse the views and opinions set forth here or in works referenced within this publication, nor can we guarantee technical and grammatical correctness. Langham Partnership does not accept any responsibility or liability to persons or property as a consequence of the reading, use or interpretation of its published content.

This work is the fruit of a life that has exhibited the Spirit's power in witness, preaching, and in teaching students who will be the next generation of Spirit-empowered preachers. This is a voice worth hearing on the topic of Spirit-empowered witness.

Dr. Gambo's observation of a lack of attention on the Holy Spirit in the contemporary church in general, and the dearth of books dealing with the critical nature of the Spirit in preaching, forms the genesis of this work. If the power of the Spirit was *the* essential ingredient in the words and deeds of Jesus and the apostles, then how much more crucial is it in contemporary preaching.

In taking up the challenge to speak into the void, Dr. Gambo has made a significant contribution to the topic. He provides a study of Spirit-empowered witness in four critical texts in Luke-Acts: Jesus's synagogue sermon in Luke 4:14–30; Jesus's encounter with the two on the Road to Emmaus in Luke 24:13–35; Luke's opening in Acts 1:1–5; and Peter's preaching in the home of Cornelius in Acts 10:34–43. He offers a detailed exegesis of each of the four passages from the original Greek, modeling a totally contextual reading of each text: historical, literary, textual, and theological. Each section concludes with insightful "Implications for Preaching." The result of his close exegesis is a tightly argued theology of preaching with a focus on Holy Spirit empowerment. Anyone who might be interested in preaching with power and permanence should take up this book and read.

**Bobby Kelly, PhD**
Ruth Dickinson Professor of Religion
Chair, Hobbs School of Theology and Ministry,
Oklahoma Baptist University, USA

Arguing that Spirit-empowered preaching is characterized by Spirit-words and Spirit-works, Dr. Gambo's research on a Lukan theology of preaching offers fresh insights with regard to the connection between pneumatology and proclamation. With a lucid style, he analyzes Jesus's own testimony about his ministry as well as the testimony of two disciples about the words and works of Jesus. Additionally, Gambo addresses the testimonies of Luke and Peter regarding the ministry of Jesus. Drawing from these testimonies, he proceeds to propose a distinct theology of Spirit-empowered preaching. Concerning the crucial role of the Holy Spirit in preaching, Dr. Gambo concludes that the Spirit's manifested presence in the life and proclamation of the preacher lead to a visitation of God among his people through the person and work of Jesus Christ.

**Matthew McKellar, PhD**
Professor of Preaching, School of Theology,
Southwestern Baptist Theological Seminary, Texas, USA

For any preacher or minister who desires to know if their ministry is empowered by the Holy Spirit, *Spirit-Empowered Witness* is a must read. David Gambo not only helps the reader identify the presence of the Holy Spirit in ministry, but outlines the conditions necessary for the Holy Spirit to empower one's preaching and ministry. Readers of *Spirit-Empowered Witness* will come away both encouraged and challenged.

**Adam D. Robinson, PhD**
Lecturer in Christian Studies,
Christian Heritage College, Brisbane, Australia

*To my father and mother,
Danjuma and Veronica Gambo*

# Contents

Preface .................................................................................................. ix

Abstract ................................................................................................. xi

Chapter 1 .............................................................................................. 1
  *Introduction*
    Definition and Rationale of Some Terms in This Study ....................... 1
    Thesis and Scope of the Study ............................................................... 4
    Methodology ........................................................................................... 6
    Contemporary Negligence to Pneumatology in Preaching .................. 7
    Contemporary Proposals on Spirit Empowerment in Preaching ........ 9
      Greg Heisler ........................................................................................ 9
      Arturo G. Azurdia III ...................................................................... 11
      James A. Forbes, Jr. ......................................................................... 13
    Contemporary Lukan Homileticians/Theologians ............................ 15
      Robert P. Menzies ............................................................................ 15
      Ronald J. Allen ................................................................................. 17
      Darrell L. Bock ................................................................................ 18

Chapter 2 ............................................................................................ 21
  *Jesus's Testimony about His Ministry: Luke 4:14–30*
    Historical Context ................................................................................ 22
    Literary Context .................................................................................... 24
    Exegesis of Luke 4:16–30 ..................................................................... 26
      The Testimony of Jesus and the Nature of His Messianic Task ..... 26
      The Empowered Prophet Mighty in Words ................................. 34
      The Empowered Prophet Mighty in Works .................................. 35
      The Response of the People in Violent Rejection ......................... 37
    Theology of the Passage ....................................................................... 38
    Conclusion: Implications for Preaching ............................................. 41

Chapter 3 ............................................................................................ 45
  *Two Disciples' Testimony about Jesus: Luke 24:13–35*
    Historical Context ................................................................................ 45
    Literary Context .................................................................................... 46
    Exegesis of Luke 24:13–35 ................................................................... 47
      The Introduction to the Narrative ................................................. 48
      The Testimony of the Two Disciples About Jesus's Ministry ....... 50

  The Exposition of the Prophet Mighty in Words and Works ....... 53
  The Result of the Exposition of the Prophet Mighty in
    Words and Works ............................................................................... 55
  Theology of the Passage ............................................................................ 56
  Conclusion: Implications for Preaching ................................................ 58

Chapter 4 ............................................................................................................ 63
 *Luke's Testimony about Jesus: Acts 1:1–5*
  Historical Context ..................................................................................... 64
  Literary Context ......................................................................................... 67
  Exegesis of Acts 1:1–5 ............................................................................... 69
   Luke's Testimony of Jesus's Ministry ............................................... 69
   Luke's Testimony of the Post-Resurrection Ministry of Jesus ....... 71
  Theology of the Passage ............................................................................ 76
  Conclusion: Implications for Preaching ................................................ 78

Chapter 5 ............................................................................................................ 83
 *Peter's Testimony about Jesus: Acts 10:34–43*
  Historical Context ..................................................................................... 83
  Literary Context ......................................................................................... 87
  Exegesis of Acts 10:34–43 ......................................................................... 88
   The Introduction to Peter's Testimony ............................................ 88
   Peter's Testimony of Jesus's Early Ministry ..................................... 90
   The Apostolic Testimony of Jesus's Later Ministry ....................... 94
   The Prophetic Testimony of the Ministry of Jesus ........................ 95
  Theology of the Passage ............................................................................ 96
  Conclusion: Implications for Preaching .............................................. 100

Chapter 6 .......................................................................................................... 105
 *Conclusion: A Theology of Spirit-Empowered Witness*
  The Divine Cause ..................................................................................... 106
  The Divine Conditions for Empowerment .......................................... 108
   There Must Be a Conversion Experience ..................................... 109
   There Must Be a Pursuit of Holiness .............................................. 110
   There Must Be a Call to Service ...................................................... 113
   There Must Be Preparation for Service .......................................... 115
   There Must Be a Commitment to Christocentric Mission ......... 119
   There Must Be a Desire to Be Empowered ................................... 120
  The Divine Consequences ...................................................................... 124
   Jesus Mighty in Words and Works .................................................. 124
   A Witness Mighty in Words and Works Today ............................. 126

Bibliography .................................................................................................... 131

# Preface

The burden to write on Spirit-empowered witness came because of the silence I noticed in the contemporary church on the Holy Spirit. Much has been written in homiletical scholarship on Christocentric preaching, genre-sensitive preaching, audience-sensitive preaching, and the mechanics of preaching. However, few books focus on the theology of preaching, especially Spirit-empowered preaching. Furthermore, I observed the high rate at which preachers are quitting ministry due to ministerial burnout and depression. Could it be that this tragedy comes from relying on human strength to carry out the Great Commission?

In reading the Gospel of Luke and the Acts of the Apostles, I was amazed with the phenomenal accomplishments of Jesus and the apostles as they fulfilled their ministries. It became apparent that the secret of Jesus and the early disciples was the power of the Holy Spirit in their lives. Thus, this work presents a theology of preaching that emphasizes the role of the Holy Spirit in preaching.

This work would not have been possible without the help of some individuals. Appreciation goes to the Gambos, Don and Lucy Lindholm, Sarah Falco, and the Hodges for their support and love. Special thanks go to my supervisor, Dr. David Allen for his encouragement and supervision. Also, thanks to Dr. Terry Wilder and Dr. Matthew McKellar for serving as my readers. My gratitude also goes to Lyndsey Huckaby and James Pence for excellent editing. I pray that this work will be a source of encouragement to those who desire to fulfill their ministry not by might nor by power, but by the power of the Holy Spirit.

David Nanchang Gambo
Fort Worth, Texas
May 2017

# Abstract

This work argues that Spirit-empowered preaching is characterized by two marks – Spirit-words and Spirit-works. Chapter 1 identifies some reasons for the contemporary negligence toward pneumatology in preaching, and reviews some contemporary homiletical/theological proposals attempting to tackle the problem. Chapter 2 analyzes Jesus's testimony about his ministry in Luke 4:14–30, where he established himself as the Spirit-empowered Messiah, mighty in words and works. Chapter 3 analyzes two disciples' testimony about Jesus in Luke 24:13–35, where they testified that Jesus was a prophet mighty in words and works. Chapter 4 analyzes Luke's testimony about Jesus in Acts 1:1–5, where Luke confirmed that his first Gospel was a summary of all that Jesus began to teach (words) and do (works). Chapter 5 analyzes Peter's testimony about Jesus in Acts 10:34–43, where Peter validates that Jesus was a prophet mighty in words and works because he was anointed by God with the Holy Spirit and power. Chapter 6 establishes a theology of Spirit-empowered preaching by harnessing all the exegetical results together in an organized pattern.

CHAPTER 1

# Introduction

The present work intends to make a contribution to the contemporary discussion of pneumatology in preaching. To be precise, I seek to construct a theology of Spirit-empowered preaching based on Luke-Acts that will model what it means to receive power to witness. I shall begin this study with definitions of terms and by reviewing some significant contributions in scholarship. Contemporary scholarship is the focal point in this study. The works of five homileticians and three Lukan theologians shall be reviewed to lay a solid foundation upon which to build.

## Definition and Rationale of Some Terms in This Study

Research of this magnitude calls for definition of key terms and a rationale for their use. Two terms that demand explicit definitions are "witness" and "empowerment." In addition to these definitions, a question may arise as to why Luke-Acts. The first term to be defined is "witness." It is worth saying at the outset that the term "witness" as used in this study takes up the biblical meaning from its root word in Greek, namely *martus*. Paul Ricoeur, in his work titled "The Hermeneutics of Testimony," traces the meaning of *martus* from the prophetic writings of the Bible and the New Testament. He arrived at a fourfold meaning:

1. The witness is not just anyone who comes forward and gives testimony, but the one who is *sent* to testify.

2. The witness does not testify about isolated and contingent facts but about the radical, global meaning of human experience. It is Yahweh himself who is witnessed to in the testimony.
3. The testimony is oriented toward proclamation . . . it is for all peoples that one people is witness.
4. Finally, witnessing implies a total engagement not only of *words* and *acts*, but also in the extreme, in the *sacrifice* of a life.[1]

This fourfold meaning of witness will be employed in this work.

In conjunction with the definition of witness, there are two rationales to support the term in this study. First, the term "witness" carries a Trinitarian ideology to preaching. Clyde E. Fant translated Dietrich Bonhoeffer's lectures on homiletics, in which the German theologian sees a Trinitarian witness. Bonhoeffer writes, "The apostles are witnesses because God is the first witness (1 John 5:9; Rom. 1:9; 1 Thess. 2:5; Phil. 1:8); because Christ is a witness (Rev. 1:5; 3:14); because the Holy Spirit is a witness (1 John 5:6)."[2] Second, several metaphors are used to describe a preacher in the Bible.[3] Of the many metaphors, three main metaphors have been distinguished in homiletical scholarship to describe a preacher, namely the herald,[4] the pastor, and the storyteller/poet.[5] All these metaphors are biblical and have their advantages

---

1. Ricoeur, "Hermeneutics of Testimony," 131. Emphasis in original.

2. Bonhoeffer, *Worldly Preaching*, 131. Also, Kevin J. Vanhoozer's words are reminiscent of Bonhoeffer's when he says,

> The concept of "witness" has rich theological connotations. The Father witnesses to the Word (1 John 5:9); Christ is the witness to God the Father; the Scriptures are a witness to Christ (Luke 24); the Spirit is the witness to the Scriptures and to Christ (1 John 5:7); the church is a witness to Word and Spirit.

See Vanhoozer, *Is There a Meaning*, 438–39.

3. John Stott identified six images: the herald, the sower, the ambassador, the steward, the pastor, and the workman. See Stott, *Between Two Worlds*, 135–36; James W. Cox identified four more. He says, "There are four words that will help us understand the nature of what we call preaching and the different ways in which the power of the Word of God comes to expression today: proclamation, witness, teaching, and prophesying." See Cox, *Preaching*, 7.

4. See Brown, *Steps to the Sermon*, 4. Also C. H. Dodd says, "A *Keryx* may be a town crier, an auctioneer, a herald, or anyone who lifts up his voice and claims public attention to some definite thing he has to announce." See Dodd, *Apostolic Preaching*, 7.

5. Robert E. C. Browne in *The Ministry of the Word* uses the analogy of a poet to speak of a preacher. See also Brueggemann, *Finally Comes the Poet*. Eugene L. Lowry says, "Preaching is storytelling. A sermon is a narrative art form." See Lowry, *Homiletical Plot*, 12.

and disadvantages.⁶ In addition to these metaphors, the imagery of a witness⁷ is also used. Since a case will be made for a theology of preaching from Luke-Acts, it would be logical to adopt the main metaphor utilized by Luke in identifying the preaching role of the apostles and the early church.

The second term to be defined is "empowerment." Whenever this term is used in this study, it refers to individuals that are called or selected and equipped by God with the power of the Holy Spirit to testify to the gospel (this definition is in accordance with Luke 24:49 and Acts 1:8).⁸ Some homileticians refer to the term as "unction," "anointing," "possession," "filling," "vitality," "endowment," and "baptism in the Spirit."⁹

Finally, why Luke-Acts? The Holy Spirit is an explicit theme in Luke-Acts.¹⁰ The witness of the apostles is harmonized with the witness of the Holy Spirit (Acts 5:32). Ju Hur, in the revised version of his dissertation, claims that "the plot of Luke-Acts is the way of witness, in seeking and saving God's people, engendered by Jesus (in the Gospel) and his witnesses (in Acts), through the

---

6. Thomas G. Long stated some advantages and disadvantages of the different metaphors of a preacher. See Long, *Witness of Preaching*.

7. In his book *Sent Forth to Preach*, Jesse Burton Weatherspoon says, "In the apostolic meaning preaching is witnessing. The preacher is a witness. The message is a testimony . . . It is the very heart of preaching that preaching is from the heart." See Weatherspoon, *Sent Forth to Preach*, 58; Walter Brueggemann, an Old Testament scholar, developed an Old Testament theology on the concept of witness and goes further to develop the idea for homiletics in his book *Cadences of Home*; Homiletician Thomas G. Long published a text on preaching as a witness. See Long, *Witness of Preaching*; Bonhoeffer, *Worldly Preaching*; Brooks, *Joy of Preaching*.

8. Acts 1:8 plays an important role in understanding the importance of empowerment. Lloyd-Jones, referring to how this verse was important to the disciples,

> They [the disciples] seem to have all the necessary knowledge, but that knowledge is not sufficient, something further is needed, is indeed essential. The knowledge indeed is vital for you cannot be witnesses without it, but to be effective witnesses you need the power and the unction and the demonstration of the Spirit in addition. Now if this was necessary for these men, how much more is it necessary for all others who try to preach these things?

See Lloyd-Jones, *Preaching and Preachers*, 308.

9. Heisler, *Spirit-Led Preaching*, 129.

10. Craig L. Blomberg says,

> The Spirit appears considerably more often in Luke than in Matthew or Mark. A characteristic expression of Luke's in both of his volumes is that someone is "filled with the Spirit," a recurring phenomenon that always leads to bold proclamation and service of the Gospel (e.g., Luke 1:15, 41; Acts 2:4; 4:31).

See Blomberg, *Jesus and the Gospels*, 169.

power and guidance of the Holy Spirit in accordance with the plan of God."[11] The Holy Spirit's empowerment for the purpose of witness and mission is obvious in the book of Acts. Peter G. Bolt says, "Through the word of his Spirit-equipped witnesses, Jesus has been and is being sent."[12] Furthermore, only the Lukan corpus allows one to see Spirit-empowered preaching prior to Jesus, with Jesus, and after Jesus. In other words, we have pre-Christ, Christ, and post-Christ in Luke-Acts. In the words of Robert P. Menzies, "The Spirit equips John for his role as the prophetic precursor, Jesus for his task as messianic herald, and the disciples for their vocation as witnesses."[13] In fact, Luke's pneumatology is more developed than the other synoptic writers. In Mark, six references were made to the Spirit, Matthew has twelve, while Luke has about twenty references in his Gospel account and more than sixty in the book of Acts.[14]

## Thesis and Scope of the Study

In this study, I seek to present a theology of Spirit-empowered preaching from Luke-Acts. This theology will assert that Spirit-empowered preaching is characterized by two marks: Spirit-words and Spirit-works. It will investigate Spirit-empowered preaching as displayed in Jesus's ministry from the testimonies of three witnesses in Luke-Acts and from the testimony of Jesus himself. This is to establish the fact that Spirit-empowered proclamation

---

11. Hur, *Dynamic Reading*, 185–86.

12. Bolt, "Mission and Witness," 195.

13. Menzies, *Empowered for Witness*, 256. This research will only focus on Jesus, the apostles, and the early church.

14. Turner, "Luke and the Spirit," 268. Turner goes on to say, there has largely been consensus among Lukan scholars on the following points: (1) of the synoptic writers, it is Luke who evinces the strongest redactional interest in the Spirit; (2) the essential background for his pneumatological material is thoroughly Jewish, deeply rooted in the Old Testament; (3) the Spirit is the uniting motif and the driving force within the Lukan salvation history and legitimizes the mission to which this leads; (4) for Luke, the Spirit is largely the "Spirit of prophecy," and in Acts especially as an "empowering for mission"; (5) correspondingly, Luke shows relatively little interest in the Spirit as the power for the spiritual, ethical, and religious renewal of the individual; (6) Luke's pneumatology develops beyond Judaism in giving the Spirit Christocentric functions: the Holy Spirit is now the "Spirit of Jesus" too (Acts 16:6–7). See Turner, "Luke and the Spirit."

(words) has power and permanence.¹⁵ As Richard Lischer writes, "In the New Testament, Jesus' word carries that kind of performative authority – not only in its reliance upon the sacred texts, but in its power to change lives and create new situations."¹⁶ This study will complement and validate exegetically the works of contemporary homileticians.

The goal of this study is to define for the contemporary preacher what it means to be Spirit-empowered and how the preacher/teacher can seek the power of the Spirit in their ministry. A proper theology of preaching has a positive impact in one's philosophy of preaching. In a nutshell, this is a theology of Spirit empowerment that fuses together the impact the Spirit has on the preacher's delivery (words) and the result (works) of the words in the congregation. For the sake of clarity, Spirit-words mean the Spirit inspiring the content of the message and granting boldness in proclamation. Spirit-works mean the Spirit transforming lives through missions. Thus, the Spirit's anointing is not only in words but also in the workings of the words. A theology that will bring together the *illocutionary* and *perlocutionary* acts of the preacher's words.¹⁷

---

15. Also, Bonhoeffer says, "Through the Holy Spirit, the incarnate Word comes to us from the Scripture in the sermon. And it is one and the same Word: the Word of creation, the Word of the Incarnation, the Word of the Holy Scripture, the Word of the sermon. It is the creating, accepting, and reconciling Word of God, for whose sake the world exists." See Bonhoeffer, *Worldly Preaching*, 129.

16. Lischer, *Theology of Preaching*, 53. Lischer goes on to describe the permanence of words from a Semitic point of view. He says every Sunday school child asks why, when Isaac discovered that he had spoken a blessing over the wrong child, he did not simply "take it back." He could not; the word spoken became the deed done. See Lischer, *Theology of Preaching*, 53. Also, Rudolf Bultmann echoes similar words, he says, "All the activity of Jesus is centered in the Word; his works are his words; his words are his works. When he does his Father's will and consummates his work, that work is his speaking the Word, his witnessing to what he has heard and seen with the Father." See Bultmann, "Concept of the Word," 308.

17. J. L. Austin developed the concept of *locutionary*, *illocutionary*, and *perlocutionary* acts of words. According to Anthony C. Thiselton, Austin defined these, respectively, as (i) a *locutionary* act of speaking which is "roughly equivalent to uttering a certain sentence with a certain sense and reference"; (ii) *illocutionary* acts such as informing, ordering, warning, undertaking (i.e. utterances which have a certain [conventional] force); and (iii) *perlocutionary* acts: namely, "what we bring about or achieve by saying something, such as convincing, persuading, deterring." See Thiselton, *New Horizons*, 293.

## Methodology

This research intends to be exegetical in approach. A proper exegetical work is a product of grammatical, syntactical, lexical, historical, and literary analysis of a passage.[18] From Luke-Acts, four selected texts will be examined for meaning and implications for a theology of preaching. These texts are Luke 4:14–30 (Jesus's testimony);[19] Luke 24:13–35 (two disciples' testimony);[20] Acts 1:1–5 (Luke's testimony);[21] and Acts 10:34–43 (Peter's testimony).[22] In the first text, Jesus testified about his empowerment. The three other texts affirm Jesus's testimony about his empowerment from the lips of other witnesses. According to the Bible, in the mouth of two or three witnesses an issue is established (2 Cor 12:1). These texts will be treated in chronological order as they appear in the Lukan corpus. As to the relationship between the Gospel of Luke and the book of Acts, this study will assume the authorship of Luke for both volumes.[23] The texts will be critically analyzed from the original Greek

---

18. Gordon D. Fee believes that good exegetical questions fall into two basic categories: questions of content (what is said) and of context (why it is said). He goes on to say that the contextual questions are of two kinds: historical and literary. The questions of content are basically of four kinds: textual criticism, lexical data, grammatical data, and historical-cultural background. See Fee, *New Testament Exegesis*, 5.

19. Hur titled this text as Jesus's witness in Galilee. See Hur, *Dynamic Reading*, 192. Also, Darrell L. Bock sees in this pericope an outline of Jesus's ministry. He goes on to say that every reader faces a choice upon reading this account: to identify with Jesus and his message of hope or to side with those who reject Jesus. See Bock, *Luke 1:1–9:50*, 420. Joel B. Green says, "The narrative has narrowed the spotlight on Jesus as the anointed one, the regal, prophetic figure who will work under the guidance of, and as empowered by, the Spirit of the Lord." See Green, *Theology of the Gospel*, 77–78. David E. Garland divides the Nazareth episode into three: the introduction as Jesus returns to Galilee and enters the synagogue in Nazareth and is asked to read in the service (4:14–17); the presentation of Jesus's reading of the Scripture, his teaching (4:18–21), and the positive reaction to it (4:22); Jesus's elaboration (4:23–27) and the violent reaction to it (4:28–30). See Garland, *Luke*, 191.

20. I. Howard Marshall says that one of the purposes of this story is to emphasize that the risen Lord appeared to witnesses and was recognized to be Jesus. See Marshall, *Gospel of Luke*, 891.

21. F. F. Bruce says, "These five verses provide a connection between the two parts of Luke's history, and partly summarize the closing scenes of the Gospel." See Bruce, *Acts of the Apostles*, 97. Bock sees this section as a review of Book 1 to the ascension. See Bock, *Acts*, 51.

22. According to Hur, Acts 8:1–11:18 is a plot that shows the disciples witnessing in Judea and Samaria. Hur, *Dynamic Reading*, 193. Craig S. Keener says, "Peter recounts here the nucleus of Jesus's the same story preached at greater length by Luke's Gospel." See Keener, *Acts 3:1–14:28*, 1794.

23. I am assuming the authorship of the two volumes to be Luke. Bock writes, "Early church tradition has consistently named Luke as the author of these volumes. Justin (*Dialogues* 103.19), the Muratorian Canon, Irenaeus (*Against Heresies* 3.1.1; 3.14.1), the so-called Anti-Marcionite Canon and Tertullian (*Against Marcion* 4.2.2; 4.5.3) name Luke as the author."

text. In addition, biblical critical resources and procedure will be employed in this research. Conclusions will be drawn at the end of every analysis.

## Contemporary Negligence to Pneumatology in Preaching

Contemporary homileticians have noticed the silence in the church about the Holy Spirit. Some have given reasons for this silence. For the sake of brevity only two will be examined here. In her article "Holy Spirit and Preaching," Cheryl Bridges Johns traces three causes of the neglect of pneumatology in theology and in preaching. First, she believes that Protestant Christianity is decidedly Christ-centered when it is not anthropocentric. Hence preaching of the word as a witness to Christ is often the hallmark of homiletics, which makes it difficult for pastors to emphasize Trinitarian theology.[24] Next, she believes that the stress on the Holy Spirit is often associated with enthusiastic forms of religion and emotive worship over and against a more rational and volitional emphasis.[25] She goes on to say "Holy Spirit shyness" is often preferred over Holy Spirit fanaticism.[26] The third reason is that "preaching is often put over against sacrament. Because of this dichotomy the act of preaching is

---

See Bock, *Luke*, 17. In addition, virtually all scholars today affirm that the same person wrote both books. D. A. Carson and Douglas J. Moo with other scholars see a considerable degree of thematic unity. They say, Luke-Acts together shows how God has acted in history to fulfill his promises to Israel and to create a world-wide body of believers drawn from Jews and Gentiles. The focus on Jerusalem in both Luke and Acts conveys this movement.

> As Luke in the gospel emphasizes (more than the other gospels) the movement toward Jerusalem (e.g., 9:51; 13:33; 17:11), the book of Acts conveys a movement away from Jerusalem. Luke thereby shows how Jesus fulfills God's plan for Israel as the basis for a movement out from Israel to embrace the entire world. Other specific themes, such as salvation, the activity of the Holy Spirit, and the power of the Word of God, run through both books.

See Carson and Moo, *Introduction to the New Testament*, 202.

24. Johns, "Holy Spirit and Preaching," 460–61.

25. Johns, 461.

26. Johns, 461. Actually, the term "Holy Spirit shyness" is originally from James Forbes, Jr., in his Lyman Beecher Lectures of 1986 at Yale Divinity School, where he says, "But many Christians are Holy Spirit shy." See Forbes, *Holy Spirit & Preaching*, 21. Forbes goes on to say,

> For some, conversations about empowerment of the Spirit in one's ministry are occasions of anxiety and intimidation. Some preachers hesitate to speak of the Spirit in relationship to what they do. Others talk about the Spirit in traditional language of faith, but without personal meaning. Hence, many of the biblical provisions for

stripped of the Spirit-endued mystery found in the liturgy."[27] Undoubtedly, these causes have deprived the church of understanding the full ministry of the Holy Spirit. If the church will rediscover the exquisite ministry of the Spirit again, it would have to start with the preachers.

William H. Willimon, professor of preaching at Duke Divinity School, in his article "Overcoming Pentecost in Our Preaching: Proclamation Without Spirit" responded to the question posited to him by a layperson at Duke Chapel as to why they seldom hear sermons about the Holy Spirit.[28] In response, Willimon states his belief that control is one of the chief functions of clergy and, based on his experience, the Holy Spirit comes to take control. He writes, "The Holy Spirit, in my dealings with him, or her, tends to be pushy, assertive, antagonistic, and imperialistic. It is the nature of the Holy Spirit to want to take over wherever he, or she, intrudes."[29] Therefore, for fear of losing control, he believes many pastors prefer to work alone.

In a similar manner, a preaching student at Duke Divinity School in one of Willimon's classes, "The Rhetoric of Preaching," asked why they had not considered the Holy Spirit's role in preaching as opposed to Aristotle?[30] Willimon responded somewhat satirically that the reason Aristotle's thought on rhetoric dominated the course was to lead the students to self-sufficiency. Since Aristotle did not believe in God, he was able to demonstrate that with proper technique, the right argument, and a skillful analysis of the audience, we will not need to ask for outside help.[31] He says, "This course is training in how to preach in such a way that one might preach so well, so skillfully and effectively, that one will not need God to make it work."[32]

---

Holy Spirit empowerment often are left unrealized like unclaimed packages or unopened letter.

Forbes, 21–22.

27. Johns, "Holy Spirit and Preaching," 461.
28. Willimon, "Overcoming Pentecost," 31.
29. Willimon, 31.
30. Willimon, 32.
31. Willimon, 32.
32. Willimon, 32. He goes on sarcastically to offer six guidelines for preachers who wish to preach without risking intrusions by the Holy Spirit: (1) Use historical criticism in studying the Scripture for preaching. (2) Write out your sermons, every word. (3) Use a great deal of sermon time explaining, defining, and explicating. (4) Try to limit your preaching to upwardly mobile, predominately white, economically prosperous congregation. (5) If you must get "spiritual" (for that sort of thing is all the rage these days, particularly among the young) just keep it as

Thankfully, some homileticians have identified some causes of the silence in the pulpit about the Holy Spirit. Others went ahead to make some proposals to tackle this indifference in contemporary homiletics. A plethora of scholarly contributions have been made in homiletics toward audience-sensitivity and genre-sensitivity, but few have been done on Spirit empowerment in evangelical scholarship.[33] Nonetheless, some homileticians have made attempts or proposals regarding the Holy Spirit's empowerment in preaching. What is Spirit-empowered preaching? We now turn to examine the works of three scholars to answer this question.

## Contemporary Proposals on Spirit Empowerment in Preaching

### Greg Heisler

Greg Heisler, professor of preaching at Southeastern Baptist Theological Seminary, in his award-winning book *Spirit-Led Preaching* laments the fact that homiletics has not been connected with pneumatology. He goes on to espouse a homiletical approach that knits together the word of God and the Spirit. Heisler titled the last chapter of his book "The Holy Spirit and the Anointing: Understanding the Spirit's Empowerment for Preaching"; this is the part that resonates most with this research. First, he begins by identifying that the anointing is the most confusing and controversial subject related to the Holy Spirit and preaching.[34] Second, he affirms that although discrepancies exist in terminologies used to describe the anointing, they all are making references to the Spirit's supernatural power attending the preaching of the word.[35] In addition to the many nuances existing in its description, he also sees disagreement in terms of definition. Some define the anointing in terms

---

"the spirit" rather than "the Holy Spirit." (6) Serve grape juice than wine at the Lord's Supper. I do not endorse all these guidelines, especially the last on his list. See Willimon, "Overcoming Pentecost," 32–34.

33. For audience-sensitive preaching, Craddock, *As One Without Authority*; Buttrick, *Captive Voice*. For genre-sensitive preaching, Arthurs, *Preaching with Variety*; Davis, *Design for Preaching*; Smith, *Recapturing the Voice*; Akin, Allen, and Mathews, *Text-Driven Preaching*; and Long, *Preaching*. For Spirit-sensitive preaching see Heisler, *Spirit-Led Preaching*; Ramm, *Witness of the Spirit*.

34. Heisler, *Spirit-Led Preaching*, 127.

35. Heisler, 129.

of result, others in terms of effect upon the preacher, others in terms of impact on the congregation, and yet others deny its existence. For Heisler, denying the existence of the anointing is tantamount to denying Scripture and history.

Heisler then goes on to affirm the existence of the anointing for preaching and he grounds it on the Spirit-filled life. He prefers using the term empowerment as an alternative to the anointing for two reasons. First, he writes, "Terms such as anointing and *Spirit filled* are unsatisfying because all believers are Spirit-filled and anointed in the biblical sense."[36] Second he says, "Empowerment seems to be broad enough to capture the dynamic of the Spirit's power for preaching and avoids the confusion and apprehension created by the stereotyped term *anointing*."[37] Heisler would say that to be empowered by the Holy Spirit means that we are filled and controlled by the Spirit, which will result in preaching that comes out of the heart and mind.[38] He goes on to list some characteristics of the Spirit's empowerment grounded on Scriptures and the experiences of various preachers. Heisler identifies freedom, vitality, power, and possession as characteristics of the Spirit's empowerment. Finally, he describes on how one can receive the Spirit's empowerment through factors like prayer, fullness, faith, humility, and weakness. He also warns of possible hindrances to the Spirit's empowerment.

Overall, after a perusal of Heisler's list of characteristics of the Spirit's empowerment in preaching, it becomes obvious that these are directed towards the spoken words of preachers. This implies that Spirit-empowered preaching brings about freedom, vitality, power, and possession to the preacher's words. In other words, Heisler is affirming the group of scholars who define the Spirit's empowerment in terms of its effect on the preacher's delivery.[39] What about the impact of the Spirit's empowerment on the congregation during preaching? Or what about the anointing in terms of its results? Undoubtedly Heisler would affirm that the Spirit also works in the congregation as well,

---

36. Heisler, 135.

37. Heisler, 135.

38. Hesiler, 137.

39. According to Heisler, there are three different ways of defining the anointing of the Spirit in scholarship; some tend to define the anointing in terms of its results, others in terms of its effect upon the preacher's delivery, and others in terms of its impact on the congregation. See Heisler, 129.

however, he primarily emphasizes the preacher's dimension in his theology of empowerment.

## Arturo G. Azurdia III

In his book *Spirit Empowered Preaching* Arturo G. Azurdia III, professor of pastoral mentoring at Western Seminary, presents a biblical theology of Spirit-empowered preaching. He believes that the efficacious empowerment of the Spirit of God is indispensable to the ministry of proclamation.[40] Besides arguing for the right message and method, the author goes on to argue for the appropriate means, which is the *sine qua non* of gospel proclamation, namely, the power of the Holy Spirit.[41] Azurdia summarized his work by three statements: (1) Spirit-empowered preaching is the principle means of advancing the kingdom of Jesus Christ; (2) Spirit-empowered preaching will be evangelical in emphasis; and (3) Spirit-empowered preaching is the responsibility of the church.

A major contribution of Azurdia's work that applies to this study is his recognition of the connection between the Spirit/work (impact on hearers) and Spirit/word (impact on preacher) relationship. He goes beyond Heisler to fuse not only word/Spirit, but also work/Spirit in his theology. In his first chapter, titled "The Greater Works," he uses Luke-Acts to support his claim that the anointing was given to bring about greater works among the people. He traces measurable results of the Spirit's empowered witnessing in the book of Acts. He uses many texts in Acts (Acts 2:41; 4:4; 5:14; 6:1; 9:31; 9:35; 9:42; 11:24; 12:24; 3:48:49; 14:1; 16:5; 17:4; 17:11–12; 18:8; and 19:20) to validate his claim.[42]

As to the word/Spirit, he writes, "A specific phrase in Luke-Acts appears eight times and always is relationship to a prophetic kind of speaking . . . the phrase can be rendered: 'filled with the Holy Spirit,' or 'having been filled with the Holy Spirit.'"[43] The first was in relationship to the birth of John the Baptist announced by the angel Gabriel (Luke 1:13–15). The seven remaining

---

40. Azurdia III, *Spirit Empowered Preaching*, 13.
41. Azurdia III, 98.
42. Azurdia III, 24–26.
43. Azurdia III, 102–3.

occurrences of the phrase (Luke 1:39–41; 42–45; Acts 2:2–4; 4:8; 4:31; 9:17; and 13:8–11) referred to the proclamation of inspired words.[44]

One problem I identified with Azurdia's work was in his approach of the Spirit/work relationship. For Azurdia, the effect of the Spirit's work is seen only in the elect. He says,

> What effects can we expect to see when the proclamation of the gospel is attended by the power of the Spirit? In part, sinners, previously unable to respond in any positive fashion, now readily embrace Jesus Christ for forgiveness of sins and the gift of eternal life . . . The elect are distinguished as those to whom the gospel comes in power.[45]

A Calvinist approach to theology is in view here.[46] If one sees the Spirit's work only when there is a positive response, then preaching that receives a negative response would not be considered Spirit-empowered preaching. In that case, Jesus's first sermon in Nazareth in Luke 4, which resulted in his rejection

---

44. Azurdia III, 104–6. In sum, Azurdia says,

> What is this "Spirit-filling"? An examination of these eight passages reveal it to be an instantaneous, sudden, and sovereign operation of the Spirit of God coming upon a man so that his proclamation of Jesus Christ might be attended by holy power. This, then, appears to be the emphasis of Paul's words when he says to the Corinthians: "And my message and my preaching were not in persuasive words of wisdom, but in demonstration of the Spirit and power" (1 Cor. 2:4). The Spirit, by the means of His power, through the words of a preacher, establishes, verifies, and confirms the gospel in the heart of a man so that he must respond to the truth he hears.

See Azurdia III, 107.

45. Azurdia III, 121.

46. In Reformed theology, the elect are the only ones that the word of God comes with saving power. R. C. Sproul writes, "To be sure, the Reformed doctrine of predestination teaches that all the elect are indeed brought to faith. God insures that the conditions necessary for salvation are met." Sproul, *Chosen by God*, 155. Also, to be brought to faith, Sproul means God gives saving faith to the elect only. He writes,

> The faith by which we are saved is a gift. When the apostle says it is not of ourselves, he does not mean that it is not our faith. Again, God does not do the believing for us. It is our own faith but it does not originate with us. It is given to us. The gift is not earned or deserved. It is a gift of sheer grace.

Sproul, 119. I concur with Norman L. Geisler, in *Chosen but Free*, that faith is not a gift only to the elect. Geisler evaluated all the verses used by Calvinists to support their claim that faith is a gift only to the elect, and concluded that it is untrue and misleading. He writes, "Nowhere does the Bible teach that saving faith is a special gift of God only to a select few. Further, everywhere the Bible assumes that anyone who wills to be saved can and does exercise saving faith." Geisler, *Chosen but Free*, 237.

when he was almost thrown down the mountain, was not Spirit-empowered. Furthermore, I am perplexed that Azurdia would present so many passages in Acts displaying the many conversions; however, he appeared oblivious to the many other passages about rejections despite of the proclamation of the word with the Spirit's empowerment. Nonetheless, Azurdia's affirmation of the relationship of Spirit/word and Spirit/work is worth noting.

## James A. Forbes, Jr.

Fondly called "the preacher's preacher," James A. Forbes, Jr. in his Lyman Beecher Lectures at Yale University of 1986, published as *The Holy Spirit and Preaching*, offers a significant contribution to the enrichment of preaching. His lectures had a dual purpose: to promote a comprehensive ecumenical conversation on the renewal of the church in the power of the Holy Spirit, and to show how contemporary preaching can be enriched by a fresh appropriation of the power of the Holy Spirit.[47] Simply put, he says, "The anointing of the Holy Spirit is the central paradigm for our discussion. It is a biblical category with rich experiential meaning."[48] In chapter 1, he presents the anointing of the Spirit in the life of Jesus as a model for the preaching ministry. In chapters 2 and 3, he demonstrates using his model the difference the anointing can make in preaching in terms of both concept and content. And in his last chapter, he describes how the anointing would revitalize the contemporary church.

Interestingly, his model of the Spirit's anointing was from the Gospel of Luke. Forbes's model plays a vital role if one is to understand the anointing. He addresses the misconceptions about the nature of the anointing in a preacher's life. For Forbes, the anointing is a process rather than a one-time event. He says, "In the light of our discussion, the anointing of the Holy Spirit is that process by which one comes to a fundamental awareness of God's appointment, empowerment, and guidance for the vocation to which we are called as the body of Christ."[49] Apart from the nature of the anointing in the life of the preacher, he writes about the manner of the anointing, which transcends the preacher's experience. He says, "Preaching under the anointing of the Spirit deeply touches the hearer, evoking either acceptance or rejection of the

---

47. Forbes, *Holy Spirit and Preaching*, 14.
48. Forbes, 16.
49. Forbes, 37.

gospel."⁵⁰ Next, he states some marks of the Holy Spirit's anointing; these are willing to witness, guidance, and power from on high. What exactly does he mean by "power from on high?" He clarifies it by saying, "The person who is anointed will experience a plus factor as he or she works for the kingdom. This edge is necessary to do the work of God effectively."⁵¹ And the work of God has to do with promoting the kingdom with signs and wonders following.⁵² Anointed preaching does not only affect the preacher, but it also generates response from the congregation. This response is either positive or negative. The Spirit empowers the words of the preacher to generate stupendous work (response in the lives of the congregation).

From the contributions of these homileticians, it is appropriate to fuse together all the findings in this survey to establish a theology of Spirit-empowered witness. Four things define Spirit-empowered witness. First, the empowerment of Jesus is the model par excellence of Spirit-empowered preaching. Second, the Holy Spirit comes upon a witness to fill and control their life implying that the Spirit controls every aspect of the preacher's life, including sermon preparation. Third, the Spirit's empowerment impacts the preacher's delivery bringing about freedom of expression, vitality, and boldness in the preaching event. Finally, the Spirit's empowerment not only impacts the preacher's delivery but also evokes a response from the congregation. The response may be positive or negative (salvation, encouragement, rejection, healing, joy, etc.).

Thus, if Jesus's empowerment is the model for Spirit-empowered preaching, then according to Luke, words and works are the two marks of Spirit empowerment. James B. Shelton writes,

> Because of his Spirit-anointing, Jesus became "mighty in deed and words" (24:19; Acts 10:38). Both his works and words were evidence that he was God's prophet. Luke sees the "mighty works and wonders and signs which God did through him" (Acts 2:22) as paradigmatic for Jesus's ministry. For this reason, Luke

---

50. Forbes, 42.
51. Forbes, 49–50.
52. Forbes, 50. Also by signs and wonders he means, the wisdom and knowledge of the human situation and the power to administer the abundant life point to uncommon dimensions of grace. The capacity to encounter principalities and powers, to cast out demons, to heal the sick and raise the dead require some special accounting. See Forbes, 50.

characterizes Jesus's ministry as endowed with Spirit-words and Spirit-works in his two strategic summaries of salvation history: the beginning of Jesus's public ministry and the beginning of the mission to the Gentiles (4:18–19; Acts 10:38).[53]

A need exists to validate this claim exegetically. That is where I seek to make a contribution. Attempting to contribute to this discussion from Luke-Acts demands that one listen to biblical theologians in this field. Is the Holy Spirit and witness a theme in the Lukan corpus? To answer this question, we will examine the works of three theologians.

## Contemporary Lukan Homileticians/Theologians
### Robert P. Menzies

Robert P. Menzies's doctoral dissertation was published in 1991 as *The Development of Early Christian Pneumatology*.[54] It was later republished in 1994 as *Empowered for Witness: The Spirit in Luke-Acts*. It was an attempt to reconstruct Luke's contribution to the development of early Christian pneumatology. Menzies's work has a dual purpose. First, he begins by challenging scholars who affirmed continuity between the soteriological activity of the Spirit, which is so prominent in Pauline corpus, with Luke's pneumatology. Menzies writes, "I shall seek to establish that Luke never attributes soteriological functions to the Spirit and that his narrative presupposes a pneumatology which excludes this dimension."[55] Second, he goes on to distinguish Luke's prophetic pneumatology from the "charismatic" perspective of the primitive church.[56]

Menzies, arguing that Luke was influenced by the dominant Jewish perception, consistently portrays the gift of the Spirit as a prophetic endowment that enables its recipient to participate effectively in the mission of God. He goes on to say,

---

53. Shelton, *Mighty in Word*, 81. In similar manner, Leo O'Reilly writes, "Like the O.T. prophetic word, the word of Jesus is dianoetic and dynamic, it has an intelligible content, a teaching, but it also produces concrete effects." See O'Reilly, *Word and Sign*, 39.
54. Menzies, *Development of Early Christian Pneumatology*.
55. Menzies, *Empowered for Witness*, 44.
56. Menzies, 45.

Although the primitive church, following in the footsteps of Jesus, broadened the functions traditionally ascribed to the Spirit in first-century Judaism and thus presented the Spirit as the source of miracle-working power (as well as prophetic inspiration), Luke resisted this innovation. For Luke, the Spirit remained the source of special insight and inspired speech.[57]

Reading through the Lukan corpus, one would struggle to agree with Menzies's claim that Luke resisted the influence of the primitive church's view on the Spirit. To say that Luke views the Spirit's role in prophetic utterance only is a narrow view of Lukan pneumatology. In fact Menzies says, "Luke, in accordance with the primitive church, does not present reception of the Spirit as necessary for one to enter into and remain with the community of salvation."[58] Should one think that Luke affirms that people can become members of the kingdom without the Spirit's regeneration?

William P. Atkinson, coming from the same Pentecostal tradition, affirms Menzies's work but rejects his narrow view of the Spirit's functions in Lukan pneumatology.[59] Indeed, Luke was focusing more on missions, but Atkinson considers it presumptuous to claim that Luke's pneumatology is that narrow. Despite Menzies's narrow view of Luke's pneumatology, he made a great contribution to this discussion. He proposed that one of the reasons why Luke wrote was to offer theological and methodological direction for the ongoing Christian mission, which explains Luke's emphasis on the validity

---

57. Menzies, 45.

58. Menzies, 227.

59. Atkinson, *Baptism in the Spirit: Luke-Acts and the Dunn Debate*, surveyed some scholarly works including a review and critique on Menzies's work. He sees Menzies's thesis that New Testament pneumatologies developed along disparate lines, meaning that Luke's view of the Spirit was neither identical to the pneumatology visible in his sources, such as Mark's Gospel and Q, nor identical to what emerges from Paul's letters or later writings. Luke's view of the Spirit was remarkably narrow, distinctive for what it excluded: for Luke, the Spirit did not grant recipients new life; did not enable them to perform miracles; did not have significant ethical impact; and is not primarily benefit these recipients at all – the Spirit was given for others. What the Spirit was given for was entirely prophetic: primarily the missionary witness of the growing church. Unsurprisingly, given such a narrow view of the Spirit's function in Lukan pneumatology, Menzies's position lies at the opposite extreme to that of Dunn, even further away from Dunn in the spectrum than Stronstad is. While there are elements of Menzies's thesis with which it is possible to disagree, he has made a great contribution to the whole discussion and no student of Lukan pneumatology can afford to ignore what he has written. See Atkinson, *Baptism in the Spirit*, 47–48.

of the mission (work) to the Gentiles, and the necessity of the Spirit's enabling.[60] With this in mind, we turn to the next theologian for more insight into Luke-Acts.

## Ronald J. Allen

In his book *Preaching Luke-Acts* Ronald J. Allen, professor of preaching and New Testament at Christian Theological Seminary, presents a thematic approach to preaching Luke and Acts. By theme he means ideas, images, associations, expressions, practices, or values that span Luke 1 through Acts 28. He writes, "A theme is introduced in Luke and then developed through Luke and Acts."[61] The title of chapter 4 is "Preaching on the Holy Spirit." He researched the role of the Spirit in Judaism, the primitive church, and contemporary church settings. Based on his Old Testament studies and other literature in Judaism, he concludes that the Spirit operates in five ways in Judaism, all of which recur in the Lukan author's two volumes. These are, (1) the Spirit is a divine tool in creation and re-creation; (2) the Spirit is universally present sustaining the world; (3) the Holy Spirit fills or anoints people; (4) the Spirit empowers persons for specific tasks; and (5) the Spirit builds communities leading to apocalypticism, which is a sign of eschatological consummation.[62]

Allen believes that Luke wrote in such a way to suggest that the Spirit works in the church and world today as very much as he worked in the worlds of Jesus and the early Christian communities. He writes, "What do we have in this story? A picture of the Spirit-filled life. A Spirit who fills, who empowers for actions of renewal, who brings the word of God to expression, who is an assuring presence in times of struggle. This Spirit is still active today."[63] Unlike Menzies, Allen affirms a broader view about the Holy Spirit in Luke-Acts.

## Darrell L. Bock

Darrell L. Bock is research professor of New Testament studies at Dallas Theological Seminary. In chapter 9 of his groundbreaking work *A Theology of Luke and Acts*, he writes about the Holy Spirit in Luke-Acts. He says, "In

---

60. Menzies, *Empowered for Witness*, 227–28.
61. Allen, *Preaching Luke-Acts*, 1.
62. Allen, 72–73.
63. Allen, 85.

this chapter, I will note both narrative sequence in references to the Spirit and do synthetic work as well."[64] Bock traces the work of the Spirit in Luke's infancy material, the body of Luke's Gospel, and in the book of Acts. In summary, he writes,

> So what does the Spirit do? The short answer is many things. He anointed Jesus and energized his birth (Luke 1:35; Acts 3:21–22; 4:16–18; 10:38). He is the giver of dreams and visions (2:17; 7:55–56). He gives revelatory words and inspires Scripture (1:2; 1:16; 4:25; 7:51; 28:25). He gives wisdom and discernment (Luke 21:15; Acts 5:3; 6:3, 5, 10; 9:31; 13:9; 16:18). He leads into praise for what God has done (Luke 1:67; Acts 2:4; 10:46; 19:6). He leads into witness (Acts 1:4, 8; 4:8; 31; 5:32; 6:10; 9:17), as well as teaching (9:31; 13:52).[65]

In a nutshell, it was the Spirit that launched Jesus's ministry and that same Spirit that ushered in a new community empowered for mission. This implies that the same Spirit empowers witnesses today.

Now, what implications can be drawn from what Lukan theologians have said about the Holy Spirit? First, they agree that the Holy Spirit is a major theme in Luke-Acts.[66] Second, they agree that the Holy Spirit empowers witnesses for proclamation of the Gospel. Third, they all agree that the Holy Spirit is presently active today as he was in the Old Testament, in Jesus's ministry, and in the early church. In summary, the Spirit is active in the preaching of the word and the working of the word. Having established a theological

---

64. Bock, *Theology of Luke and Acts*, 212.
65. Bock, 226.
66. New Testament scholars affirm this as well. George E. Ladd writes,

> Even in his Gospel Luke makes more frequent mention of the Holy Spirit than do Matthew and Mark (especially in chs. 1–2); but in 24:49 the cryptic references to "the promise of my Father" and "power from above" point forward to what will be a controlling theme of Luke's second volume, which has been appropriately described as "The Acts of the Holy Spirit." Acts 1 is a time of waiting (vv. 4–8), and it is only with the coming of the Spirit at Pentecost in chapter 2 that the mission of the disciples can begin. From that time on Luke constantly emphasizes that the disciples depend on the Holy Spirit for the power to witness (e.g., 4:8, 31; 5:32; 6:10; 7:55) and that it is the Holy Spirit who directs the development of the mission (e.g., 8:29, 39; 10:19; 13:2, 4; 16:6–10). The whole operation is masterminded by the Spirit; without the Spirit, there would be no mission, no story for Luke to relate.

See Ladd, *Theology of the New Testament*, 244.

and homiletical foundation, I will now analyze four testimonies about the ministry of Jesus Christ of Nazareth. The goal is to establish the claim that Spirit-empowered preaching is demonstrated in mighty words and mighty works, and to offer some suggestions on how a contemporary preacher may seek the power of the Spirit in their ministry.

CHAPTER 2

# Jesus's Testimony about His Ministry: Luke 4:14–30

Some assumptions that will be applied to this work will be stated at the outset. First, the Gospel of Luke is the only Gospel with a sequel, namely Acts. Luke-Acts are inseparable.[1] Luke not only introduces Jesus and his ministry, but also shows how that ministry relates to the early church period.[2] Second, this research holds the balanced view proposed by I. Howard Marshall that Luke is both a historian and theologian, and that the best term to describe

---

1. Robert Maddox writes,

    Today most workers in this field accept it as proven; and one recent, major review of the history of Lucan studies actually concludes that the primary gain of the recent criticism of Luke-Acts has been the recognition that the Gospel according to Luke and the Book of Acts are really two volumes of one work, which must be considered together.

    See Maddox, *Purpose of Luke-Acts*, 3. Also, Kenneth R. Wolfe argued for a chiastic structure in Luke-Acts. Wolfe says Luke-Acts does involve ring composition and that the basic structure is as follows:

       A Galilee, Luke 4:14–9:50.
          B Journey to Jerusalem (through Samaria and Judea), Luke 9:51–19:40.
             C Jerusalem, Luke 19:41–24:49.
                D Ascension, Luke 24:50–51.
             C' Jerusalem, Acts 1:12–8:1a
          B' Judea and Samaria, Acts 8:1b–11:18.
       A' To the end of the earth, Acts 11:19–28:31.

    See Wolfe, "Chiastic Structure," 67.

2. Bock, *Luke 1:1–9:50*, 1.

him is "evangelist," a term that includes both of the others.[3] Third, as for the date of composition, it is uncertain; however, most scholars hold to a date between AD 63–100.[4] Finally, this work will not assume any source theory for the composition of Luke.[5]

This chapter presents an exegetical analysis of Luke 4:16–30. It has a three-fold purpose: (1) to establish the testimony of Jesus as one who is anointed by God to fulfill his messianic task; (2) to validate the claim that Spirit-empowered witnessing is demonstrated by Spirit-word (mighty in words) and Spirit-work (mighty in deeds); and (3) to assess the implications of the text for preaching.

## Historical Context

The historical context deals with the ancient situation behind the text. Aspects like authorship, date of writing, and author's sources have been assumed. Only recipients and purpose will be discussed. Luke's statement in Luke 1:3–4 should be given priority if one is to determine his recipients. He says, "It seemed fitting for me as well, having investigated everything carefully from the beginning, to write it out for you in consecutive order, most excellent Theophilus; so that you may know the exact truth about the things you have been taught" (Luke 1:3–4 NASB). The identity of Theophilus is not a question this research seeks to address; however, it is clear that the person in question is a person of advanced status due to the title, "most excellent." In addition,

---

3. Marshall, *Luke*, 18.

4. Advocates for date of composition sometime in the sixties are Darrell L. Bock, John Nolland, R. C. H. Lenski, Malcolm O. Tolbert, Alfred Plummer, and Howard Marshall. Advocates for the date of composition between AD 70–90 are Joseph A. Fitzmyer and David E. Garland.

5. Joseph A. Fitzmyer says,

> Practically all commentators on the Lucan Gospel are agreed that its author not only knew but made use of earlier gospel composition in his writing the story of Jesus. Rare indeed are those who would still try to explain its origin by an exclusive appeal to an earlier oral tradition. Even those who do not use the modified Two-Source Theory or the Two-Document Hypothesis tend to admit that Luke was at least dependent on Matthew. And such dependence seems to be suggested by the Lucan prologue itself . . . In the present commentary I shall posit three main sources and must, therefore, set forth some of the reasons for regarding the Lucan Gospel as dependent on the Marcan source ("MK"), the source "Q," and a source, not necessarily written, which is called "L."

See Fitzmyer, *According to Luke I-IX*, 66–67.

most commentators agree that Theophilus was not the only audience Luke intended; he wrote to an extended circle of friends and influence.[6] Furthermore, it is generally agreed that the recipients were Christians. Garland writes, "The readers are assumed to be Christians, and they also are assumed to have familiarity with Scripture and to accept its divine authority."[7]

According to Grant R. Osborne, the most important aspect in the historical context is the purpose of the book.[8] There are many theories about Luke's purpose. These theories may be broadly classified based on whether Luke's audience is to people outside the church or within it.[9] The plethora of suggestions shows the complexity involved in the issue of purpose. However, of all these suggestions, those that center on God's salvific role and the new community created as a result of God's salvation are most likely to resonate with Luke's purpose.[10] I concur with Green that Luke's aim was to write the story of the continuation and fulfillment of God's project – a story that embraces both the work of Jesus and of the followers of Jesus after his ascension.[11]

---

6. See Green, *Gospel of Luke*, 44. Also Bock writes, "Luke did not write, however, just for this one person, but for any who felt this tension. Any Gentile feeling out of the place in an originally Jewish movement could benefit from the reassurance Luke offers." See Bock, *Luke 1:1–9:50*, 15; Marshall, *Gospel of Luke*, 35.

7. Garland, *Luke*, 35. Also Maddox, Bock, Marshall, Nolland, and Green concur with Garland.

8. Osborne, *Hermeneutical Spiral*, 38.

9. For advocates that hold to an audience outside the church, there are three theories. (1) F. F. Bruce and J. C. O'Neill hold that the chief purpose of Luke-Acts is evangelism; (2) A. J. Mattill holds that Luke wrote to defend Paul at his trial; (3) B. S. Easton and E. Haenchen hold that Luke wrote to defend the Christians in the eyes of the Roman government. For advocates that hold to an audience within the church, there are four theories, (1) M. Schneckenburger and F. C. Baur hold that Luke wrote to defend Paul's memory against attacks upon it by Jewish Christians; (2) H. Conzelmann holds that Luke's purpose was to solve an alleged crisis of faith in the church, due to the delay of the parousia; (3) C. H. Talbert holds that Luke-Acts was written for the express purpose of serving as a defense against Gnosticism; (4) Finally, W. C. Van Unnik holds that Luke's work has been described as the confirmation of the gospel. See Maddox, *Purpose of Luke-Acts*, 20–22.

10. Bock, *Luke 1:1–9:50*, 14.

11. Green, *Theology of the Gospel*, 47. Also, Marshall pointed that Luke presents the story of Jesus as being the fulfillment of prophecy and indeed as being determined throughout by the will of God revealed in prophecy. The ministry is the period of fulfillment in which God's promises of salvation are realized. The keynotes sounded at the outset are the ideas of salvation and good news. The teaching, healings, and acts of compassion shown by Jesus are all parts of the proclamation of good news, and the message of Jesus, finely summed up in the saying, "The Son of man is come to seek and to save that which was lost." See Marshall, *Gospel of Luke*, 35–36.

## Literary Context

The theme of the Spirit connects Luke 3 and 4. The Spirit that came upon Jesus during his baptism (Luke 3:22) now leads him to the wilderness to triumph over the devil, thus demonstrating that he is the faithful Son of God (Luke 4:1–13). The temptation was fruitless, and Jesus returned to Galilee in the power of the Spirit to commence his task. Luke gives a brief summary of Jesus's ministry, focusing on Jesus as a popular teacher empowered by the Spirit (4:14–15).[12] Luke then records the sermon of Jesus in Nazareth (4:16–30), which has no synoptic parallels.[13] Menzies says, "The Nazareth pericope (4:16–30) not only shed light on Luke's understanding of Jesus' pneumatic anointing, but it stands as the cornerstone of Luke's entire theological program."[14] Jesus's sermon led to his rejection by his country people. In contrast to his rejection in Nazareth, the people of Capernaum accepted his ministry and attempted to restrain him from leaving their region (4:31–42).

---

12. Almost all commentators take these verses as summary statement of Jesus's Galilean ministry. Also, these verses are to be regarded as an editorial statement, composed by Luke, who differs with the Marcan source, by which he is otherwise inspired. From the form-critical point of view, they are a "summary" of the sort that Luke uses in Acts. Whereas the summaries in Acts describe (idyllically) the life of early Christians or the growth of the church in its springtime, this one gives an overview of the Galilean ministry of Jesus. See Fitzmyer, *According to Luke I–IX*, 521–22. It is also worth noting here that the Spirit, in this context, is not only characterized as guiding and inspiring Jesus to go and teach in Galilee, but also defined as God's power in relation to Jesus's activity. See Hur, *Dynamic Reading*, 212–13.

13. Many commentators have suggested reasons as to why Luke included the sermon in Nazareth, which was not included in the parallel sections in Mark and Matthew. According to Garland, it is possible that Luke has deliberately shifted and edited the incident he found in Mark 6:1–6a to include Jesus's maiden sermon. In this passage, and in Matt 13:53–58, the visit to Nazareth and his subsequent rejection occurs after an extended period of ministry, not at the beginning of his ministry. Also, Mark and Matthew do not record the synagogue's initial approbation of Jesus that turns into disapproval, only their repudiation of him. Mark concludes the incident by commenting that Jesus was unable to do any mighty work there, except heal a few people, and he marveled at their lack of faith (Mark 6:6a). Matthew's account also concludes that Jesus did not do many mighty works there because of a lack of faith (Matt 13:58). Luke records fuller details of his sermon, including the Scripture he reads. Whether Luke used Mark or an independent source, the Nazareth incident is a programmatic text for his gospel. It reveals what kind of Messiah Jesus will be. His mission brings good news and deliverance to the outcasts and oppressed. See Garland, *Luke*, 189.

14. Menzies, *Empowered for Witness*, 145. Similarly, Charles H. Talbert says that in 4:16–30 the evangelist gives a programmatic statement of Jesus's ministry – and by extension, the ministry of the church – as one empowered by the Holy Spirit, involving not only preaching, but also healing and exorcism, and moving outwards to touch the whole world. See Talbert, *Reading Luke*, 57.

Despite their tenacity, Jesus resisted and went to other cities to preach the kingdom of God (4:43–44).

Some scholars have argued for a chiastic structure in the text (4:16–30).[15] The chiastic structure is possible, but it does not cover the entire pericope (4:14–30). It only deals with 4:16–20; thus, most commentators agree that it is better to see it from the literary structure. The literary structure is held together largely by geographical orientation. Below is Bock's division:

I. Luke's preface and the introduction of John and Jesus (1:1–2:52)
II. Preparation for ministry: anointed by God (3:1–4:13)
III. Galilean ministry: revelation of Jesus (4:14–9:50)
IV. Jerusalem journey: Jewish rejection and the new way (9:51–19:44)
V. Jerusalem: the innocent one slain and raised (19:45–24:53)[16]

The argument of Luke's Gospel emerges as one proceeds through it in literary order.[17] Section III is the focus of this chapter. Talbert writes, "The dominant emphasis on the power of Jesus and the subordinate theme of the mission of the gospel to all peoples cannot be missed by an attentive reader of 4:16–9:50."[18]

The exegetical structure for this work will capture the dynamics of the narrative scenes (i.e. two major declarations and two distinct responses). Also, the structure will take into consideration the goal of this research. There

---

15. Below is Charles H. Talbert chiastic structure:

  A He stood up to read (16c)
   B there was given to him (17a)
    C opening the book (17b)
     D Isa 61:1f., plus 58:6 (18–19)
    C' closing the book (20a)
   B' he gave it back to the attendant (20b)
  A' he sat down (20c).

Talbert, *Reading Luke*, 54–55. Also see Tiede, *Luke*, 103.

16. Bock, *Luke 1:1–9:50*, 20.

17. Bock, 20.

18. Talbert, *Reading Luke*, 53. He goes on to assert that there are two main theological concerns in 4:16–9:50. In the first place, Luke wants to speak about one stage of Jesus's way. In this phase of his career, Jesus is the one who is anointed-empowered by the Holy Spirit and his activity demonstrates the kingly power of God. The accent is on power. In the second place, Luke also wants to foreshadow in Jesus's career certain facets of the later church's life. See Talbert, *Reading Luke*.

are four sections in this chapter: the testimony of Jesus and the nature of his messianic task (vv. 16–21); the empowered prophet mighty in words (v. 22); the empowered prophet mighty in works (vv. 23–27); and the response of the people in violent rejection (vv. 28–30).

## Exegesis of Luke 4:16–30

It is necessary to begin an exegetical analysis with textual criticism. According to Paul D. Wegner, textual criticism is the science and art that seeks to determine the most reliable wording of a text.[19] Textual criticism deals with "variant readings," that is any difference in wording that occurs among manuscripts.[20] Luke 4:16–21 contains two textual variants according to UBS[5]. Since the variants do not have any implication to the meaning of the text, there is no point discussing them.[21]

### The Testimony of Jesus and the Nature of His Messianic Task

> And he came into Nazareth, where he had been raised, and he entered the synagogue according to his custom on the Sabbath day, and he stood to read. And the scroll of the prophet Isaiah was given to him, and unrolling the scroll, he found the place where it was written, "The Spirit of the Lord is upon me, because

---

19. Wegner, *Student's Guide*, 24. In addition, Wegner gives a threefold importance of textual criticism. First and foremost, it attempts to establish the most reliable reading of the text. Second, in cases where a definitive reading is impossible to determine, it can help to avoid dogmatism. Third, it can help the reader better understand the significance of marginal readings that appear in various Bible translations. Textual criticism is not a matter of making negative comments or observations about the biblical text; instead it is the process of searching through the various sources of the biblical texts to determine the most accurate or reliable reading of a passage. See Wegner, 24.

20. Wegner, 24.

21. A brief comment on the variants for those interested will be sufficient. In 4:17, the participle, "unrolled" (ἀναπτύξας), is given a {B} designation. Bruce M. Metzger notes that since the synagogal copies of Old Testament books were in scroll form, the use of the verb "to unroll" is highly appropriate. He assumes that copyist may have introduced ἀναπτύξας as a pedantic correlative to πτύξας in v. 20. Therefore, ἀναπτύξας is the appropriate verb that will be used in this research. The final variant is in 4:18, following ἀπέσταλκέν με, and has a designation of {A}. Metzger says, "Following ἀπέσταλκέν με, a number of witnesses continue with the words ἰάσασθαι τοὺς συντετριμμένους τὴν καρδίαν. This is an obvious scribal supplement introduced in order to bring the quotation more completely in accord with the Septuagint text of Is 61.1." This exegesis will avoid the scribal addition. See Metzger, *Textual Commentary*, 114.

he has anointed me to proclaim good news to the poor, He has sent me to herald release to the captives and to the blind recovery of sight, to send in release to those oppressed, to herald the favorable year of the Lord." And he rolled up the scroll, gave it to the attendant, and sat down; and the eyes of all in the synagogue were looking intently at him. Then he began to speak to them, "Today this Scripture has been fulfilled in your hearing." (Luke 4:16–21)[22]

Luke begins the first clause in verse 16 by identifying Jesus's geographical location after his temptation (4:1–13), namely, Nazareth. The relative clause "where he had been raised" (οὗ ἦν τεθραμμένος) is descriptive, as it seeks to identify the town of Nazareth (a city in Galilee) with Jesus's infancy. According to Nolland, the clause is reminiscent of the infancy narrative, but it also prepares for verses 22–23.[23] Now in Nazareth, Jesus entered the synagogue "according to his custom" (κατὰ τὸ εἰωθὸς αὐτῷ) on the Sabbath day. This prepositional phrase is significant because it reflects a pattern that will also be seen in Acts. Only Luke among the synoptic evangelists stresses Jesus's habitual frequenting of the synagogue.[24] He would later write the same thing about the apostles and early Christians in Jerusalem, describing them as habitually entering the temple (Acts 2:46; 3:1; 4:1; 5:12, 42; 21:26).[25] Furthermore, Green asserts that Luke intended to depict not only Jesus's piety in synagogue attendance, but also his habit of expounding the Scriptures there (cf. Acts 17:2).[26] An infinitival clause indicating purpose was used to say, "he stood to read" (καὶ ἀνέστη ἀναγνῶναι). However, it should not be assumed that the Scriptures were read only in the synagogue without exposition.

"And when he stood to read, the scroll of the prophet Isaiah was given to him" (v. 17), the verbal clause "he found the place" (εὗρεν τὸν τόπον) indicates that Jesus deliberately sought out the passage of Isaiah 61. It makes sense then

---

22. Translations provided for exegesis are my own. Other translations for biblical references are from the NASB unless otherwise stated.

23. Nolland, *Luke 1–9:20*, 195. Also, Fitzmyer sees a foreshadowing of 4:24. See Fitzmyer, *According to Luke I–IX*, 530.

24. Nolland, *Luke 1–9:20*, 195.

25. Nolland, 195.

26. See Green, *Gospel of Luke*, 209; Marshall, *Gospel of Luke*, 181; Nolland, *Luke 1–9:20*, 195.

to assume that there was not a fixed reading in the synagogue because Jesus "found" (εὗρεν) the place in Isaiah from which he wanted to give exposition. Bock says, "If the text was part of a fixed reading schedule, then the scroll would have been opened at the appropriate place. This detail suggests that a reading schedule was not used, but that Jesus chose his text."[27]

It is important to explain some background issues about the Isaiah quotation. First, the Isaiah quotation is dependent on the Septuagint (LXX) despite some variations. In his monumental work *Jesus and the Old Testament*, R. T. France compared how Jesus applied Old Testament quotations to himself. He asserts that Luke 4:18 is a quotation from Isaiah 61:1–2, despite the variations noted in the LXX, both in agreement with the MT (Masoretic Text) and against it; the text of the quotation is basically LXX.[28] Second, in addition to affirming Luke's adherence to the Septuagint text of Isaiah 61:1–2, Menzies went on to compare the citations and identified four points of divergence. He writes that Luke 4:18–19 deviates from the text of Isaiah 61:1–2 (LXX) at four points: the phrase "to heal the brokenhearted" (ἰάσασθαι τοὺς συντετριμμένους τῇ καρδίᾳ) has been omitted; an excerpt from Isaiah 58:6 (LXX), "to set free the oppressed" (ἀπόστελλε τεθραυσμένους ἐν ἀφέσει), has been inserted in the quotation; the "announce" (καλέσαι) of the LXX has been altered to "proclaim" (κηρύξαι); and the final phrase of the LXX (καὶ ἡμέραν ἀνταποδόσεως), which refers to divine retribution, has been omitted.[29] Regardless of the variations in the citation, it should be noted that the variations did not affect the sense or the applicability of the quotation.[30]

---

27. Bock, *Luke 1:1–9:50*, 404; Robert H. Stein holds that Luke indicated that Jesus deliberately chose the following passage to read and thus emphasized his messianic consciousness as he began his ministry. See Stein, *Luke*, 155. On the contrary, some commentators believe it was a fixed passage of the day. Eduard Schweizer says, "The selection of the scroll and presumably also the text was not up to Jesus." See Schweizer, *Good News*, 88. Also E. Earle Ellis sees the probability of an assigned passage. See Ellis, *Gospel of Luke*, 97.

28. France, *Jesus and the Old Testament*, 248. Also, for an extensive discussion on text criticism and the history of the function of Isaiah 61:1–3 in Luke 4, see Evans and Sanders, *Luke and Scripture*.

29. Menzies, *Empowered for Witness*, 147.

30. See Sloan, *Favorable Year of the Lord*, 31–32; Bock concurs that none of these changes alter Isaiah's basic sense; but might indicate that Luke is summarizing textual material used by Jesus in this synagogue address, since a normal synagogue reading would not mix passages quite like this, and the description of Jesus's remarks here is decidedly brief and dramatic. See Bock, *Luke 1:1–9:50*, 405.

The purpose of the citation in the sermon by Luke is to validate scripturally the anticipation by the Israelites of the promised Messiah. Luke had already stated this expectation from the lips of Zacharias (1:68–79), Simeon (2:25–32), and Anna the prophetess (2:36–38). Jesus is the deliverer that Israel has been waiting for. France writes, "The point of the quotation in Jesus' sermon at Nazareth does not depend on the details, but on the picture as a whole. His assertion is that in himself God's appointed redeemer has come."[31] In addition, I concur with Menzies that the quotation plays an important role in the narrative because it defines with precision the significance that Luke attaches to Jesus's pneumatic anointing to carry out his messianic mission.[32]

After finding the Isaiah 61:1–2 passage, Jesus went on to read it. The quotation begins with a reference to the speaker's anointing with the Spirit of the Lord, "The Spirit of the Lord is upon me" (Πνεῦμα κυρίου ἐπ' ἐμὲ). Luke is asserting that the speaker in Isaiah is aware of the Spirit's presence in his life. How the awareness became obvious to the speaker is indicated by a causal preposition, "because" (εἵνεκεν), which can be taken as ablative of cause. James A. Brooks and Carlton L. Winbery hold that an ablative of cause is sometimes used to indicate the reason for an action.[33] The action in this case is indicated by the verbal phrase, "he anointed me" (ἔχρισέν με). The verb "anoint" (χριω) means "to rub the body or part of it," or "to stroke the body." When used with oil it means "to smear."[34] The word is used two other times by Luke (Acts 4:27; 10:38) to mean empowerment to fulfill a divine mandate.[35] The speaker of Isaiah was empowered by the Spirit of God for his messianic ministry.

---

31. France, *Jesus and the Old Testament*, 253.

32. Menzies, *Empowered for Witness*, 155–56. Menzies goes on to say, that by altering the text of Isa 61:1–2 (LXX), Luke brings the quotation into conformity with his distinctive prophetic pneumatology, thus highlighting preaching as the primary product of Jesus's anointing and the pre-eminent aspect of his mission. See Menzies, *Empowered for Witness*.

33. Brooks and Winbery, *Syntax of New Testament*, 28.

34. Friedrich, *Theological Dictionary of the New Testament* (TDNT), s.v. "χριω." Also Bauer, *Greek-English Lexicon* (BDAG), s.v. "χριω."

35. There are some Lukan scholars like Menzies who believe that the anointing of Jesus was prophetic in nature. See Menzies, *Empowered for Witness*, 45. Also, S. J. Ignace De La Potterie, wrote an article titled "The Anointing of Christ," in which he analyzed the four texts (Luke 4:18; Acts 4:27; 10:38; Heb 1:9) that speak about the anointing of Jesus. He concluded that the anointing at the ascension (Heb 1:9) is a metaphor to indicate gladness at the moment when Christ begins to exercise his royal power. As for the anointing at the baptism, by which Jesus was anointed with the Holy Spirit and with power, it was prophetic anointing. On the

Jesus would later identify himself with the speaker of Isaiah, claiming to be the Anointed One. This anointing took place during his baptism (3:22), when the Spirit of God came down "upon him" (ἐπ' αὐτόν) like a dove. Peter refers to the Jordan incident as the anointing of Jesus in Acts 10:37–38. However, the Jordan incident was not the first experience of the Spirit in Jesus's life. Luke had already declared that Jesus was Spirit conceived (1:35), and his childhood displayed the influence of the Spirit in his life (2:40–52). James D. G. Dunn in his legendary book *Baptism in the Holy Spirit* believes that "the baptism of Jesus may possibly be described as a second experience of the Spirit for Jesus; however, it is not a second experience of the new covenant, or of Jesus within the new covenant."[36] Therefore, the Spirit came upon Jesus to empower him for his messianic ministry. It is by means of the Spirit empowerment that Jesus would fulfill his ministry. Jesus would later tell his disciples to wait in Jerusalem for the empowerment of the Spirit, which was likewise the means for their effective witness (Luke 24:49). The nature of Jesus's task was marked out by four infinitival phrases indicating purpose. An infinitive of purpose indicates the aim or purpose of the action expressed by the main verb.[37]

The first purpose infinitival phrase in verse 18 is "to proclaim good news" (εὐαγγελίσασθαι). His prophetic mission is to preach the gospel. For Luke, "preach" (κηρύσσω) and "to proclaim good news" (εὐαγγελίζω) are synonymous (4:43–44; 8:1). In the Luke passage, it is not clear whether "to proclaim good news" (εὐαγγελίσασθαι) is to be taken with the preceding verb, "he anointed" (ἔχρισέν), or with the following verb, "he has sent" (ἀπέσταλκέν). The UBS[5] text went with the former because the first punctuation has the infinitival phrase with the verb, "he anointed" (ἔχρισέν). However, the MT and the LXX have the infinitival phrase punctuated with the latter verb, "he has sent" (ἀπέσταλκέν). On the grounds that Luke depended on the MT and the LXX, and since three of the four infinitival phrases follow after the latter verb ἀπέσταλκέν, we adopt the latter as the controlling verb.

---

other hand, the expression in Acts 4:27, ("thy servant whom thou didst anoint"), brings together the themes of anointing and Servant and in this way establishes a relation between the baptism and the passion. See Ignace De La Potterie, "Anointing of Christ," 182.

36. Dunn, *Baptism in the Holy Spirit*, 24–25. Furthermore, Dunn regards the descent of the Spirit on Jesus at Jordan as a baptism in the Spirit, and it cannot be denied that it was this anointing with the Spirit which equipped Jesus with power and authority for his mission to follow. Dunn, 24.

37. Brooks and Winbery, *Syntax of New Testament*, 133.

Jesus was sent to proclaim good news "to the poor" (πτωχοῖς). The term "poor" in Luke 4:18a has to do with the marginal phenomena of human society, those who are economically disadvantaged, those lacking divine resources or spiritual worth, especially the gentile world (cf. 6:20; 7:22; 14:13,21; 16:20,22; 18:22; 19:8; 21:3).[38] The point is that the speaker of Isaiah 61:1-2 is going to announce consolation to those who have been marginalized by society and are looking up to God for liberation and fellowship. Indeed, Luke recorded how Jesus brought consolation and succor to those on the fringes of society (6:18-19; 7:11-17; 7:36-50).

In the second infinitival phrase in verse 18, Jesus was also sent "to herald release to the captives" (κηρύξαι αἰχμαλώτοις ἄφεσιν). In the Old Testament, reference to captives meant the exiled, and often has spiritual overtones, especially since exile is viewed as a consequence of sin.[39] In the New Testament, the noun "release" (ἄφεσις) means God's forgiveness, especially with the genitive (Mark 1:4; Luke 1:77; Acts 2:38; 5:31; 10:43; Col 1:14). And even when ἄφεσις is meant in the sense of "liberation" as in this verse (a quotation from Isaiah 61:1 and 58:6), it at least includes the thought of forgiveness.[40] Tannehill would affirm that the verse is speaking of release of sins, but he also sees release from physical ailments that are regarded as the result of Satan's bondage (Luke 13:16; Acts 10:38).[41] Jesus is also expected to grant "recovery of sight to the blind" (τυφλοῖς ἀνάβλεψιν). One would argue for both a literal and metaphorical view. This is because in the Lukan context Jesus granted sight to a blind man at the gate of Jericho (Luke 18:35-43). In the metaphorical sense, it refers to spiritual blindness (Luke 1:78-79; 2:30-32; 6:39; Acts 9:8-18; 13:47; 22:11-13; 26:17-18).

---

38. TDNT, s.v. "πτωχος." Also, BDAG, s.v. "πτωχος." Bock sees it as "soteriological generalization," that is, it refers to those who most often responded to Jesus (1 Cor. 1:26-29). In an invitation context it refers to those who are open to God. See Bock, *Luke 1:1-9:50*, 408; Green has a broader view. He says the poor are not defined merely in subjective, spiritual or personal, economic terms, but in the holistic sense of those who are for any of a number of socio-religious reasons relegated to positions outside the boundaries of God's people. By directing his good news to these people, Jesus indicates that even these "outsiders" are the objects of divine grace. Others may regard such people as beyond the pale of salvation, but God has opened a way for them to belong to God's family. See Green, *Gospel of Luke*, 211.

39. Bock, *Luke 1:1-9:50*, 409.

40. TDNT, s.v. "ἄφεσις," by Gerhard Kittel. Also, BDAG s.v. "ἄφεσις."

41. Tannehill, *Luke*, 92.

The third infinitive in Luke 4:18, "to send in release to those oppressed" (ἀποστεῖλαι τεθραυσμένους ἐν ἀφέσει) is derived from Isaiah 58:6 in the LXX. The word "release" (ἀφέσει) appears again in this phrase like in the previous. Stein sees a synonymous parallelism with the preceding statement.[42] On the contrary, Bock sees the imagery of the year of Jubilee; indicating that Jesus's role is not only to proclaim deliverance, but also to bring that release. Thus, Jesus is seen as both eschatological prophet and Messiah.[43] Indeed, the insertion of Isaiah 58:6 was to emphasize the liberating power of Jesus's Spirit-empowered preaching.

The Isaiah 61 quotation ends with the final infinitival phrase in verse 19, "to herald the favorable year of the Lord" (κηρύξαι ἐνιαυτὸν κυρίου δεκτόν). The genitive κυρίου introduces the agent of unstated events: "the year when the Lord will show favor to his people."[44] Undoubtedly, this is an allusion to the year of Jubilee (Lev 25), which was held every fifty years. Garland noted that the Jubilee should not be taken literally, since Jesus quotes from Isaiah not Leviticus, it is more likely that he is drawing on Jubilee imagery to refer to the day of salvation.[45] This in fact is affirmed in other passages (Isa 49:8 and 2 Cor 6:2). The imagery is intended to evoke unspeakable joy over the news of emancipation from spiritual and physical bondage through the agent of God, namely, Jesus. Luke omitted the last phrase of Isaiah 61:2, "the day of vengeance of our God" (καὶ ἡμέραν ἀνταποδόσεως) because Jesus first

---

42. Stein, *Luke*, 156; Marshall also holds similar view. See Marshall, *Gospel of Luke*, 184.

43. Bock, *Luke 1:1–9:50*, 410; Menzies also holds to this view. In his analysis of the text he concluded that

> it is highly probable that: the phrase ἰάσασθαι τοὺς συντετριμμένους τῇ καρδίᾳ was omitted by Luke due to his distinctive prophetic pneumatology; due to the verbal linkage which ἄφεσις provides with the preceding phrase, Luke inserted Isa. 58:6c ἀποστεῖλαι τεθραυσμένους ἐν ἀφέσει into the text of Isa. 61:1–2 in order to emphasize the liberating power of Jesus' Spirit-inspired preaching; Luke is responsible for the alteration of καλέσαι (LXX) to κηρύξαι. This change, while reflecting Luke's emphasis on preaching as the pre-eminent activity inspired by the Spirit, is due principally to stylistic concerns.

Also, he says that Luke omitted the final phrase of Isa 61:2a (καὶ ἡμέραν ἀνταποδόσεως) in order to emphasize the salvific dimension of Jesus's work. See Menzies, *Empowered for Witness*, 155.

44. Culy, Parsons, and Stigall, *Luke*, 134.

45. Garland, *Luke*, 200; Also, Bock says, "Jubilee, by analogy, becomes a picture of total forgiveness and salvation, just as it was in its prophetic usage in Isa. 61." See Bock, *Luke 1:1–9:50*, 410.

appeared for salvation, not vengeance or judgment. Luke would later speak of Jesus's future coming for judgment in Luke 10:14; Acts 17:31; 24:25. Nolland believes that this is due to Luke's two-stage eschatology for Jesus – salvation now, judgment in the future.[46]

After Jesus had read the text, "he rolled up the scroll" (πτύξας τὸ βιβλίον), and gave it back to the attendant, who was responsible for keeping the scroll in the ark. Thereafter, Jesus "sat down" (ἐκάθισεν) to give the exposition. At this point, Jesus captured the attention of all the people in the synagogue, for Luke writes, "And the eyes of all in the synagogue were looking intently at him" (4:20). In its verb form, the participle, "looking intently" (ἀτενίζοντες) in verse 20, is a Lukan favorite. Luke uses it twelve times in Luke-Acts to express focused attention, or intense gaze of esteem (Luke 22:56; Acts 1:10; 3:4, 12; 6:15; 7:55; 10:4; 11:6; 13:9; 14:9; and 23:1). All the people were waiting in anticipation of what Jesus would say. Why were the people captivated by his reading of the Scripture? Perhaps his reputation (vv. 14–15) and the chosen text riveted the audience.[47]

Then he began to speak to them that "today this Scripture has been fulfilled in your hearing." The word "today" (Σήμερον) in verse 21 is fronted at the head of the clause for the sake of emphasis. It is also a Lukan term, used seven times in Luke's Gospel (cf. 2:11; 5:26; 12:28; 13:32–33; 19:5, 9; 33:34; 22:61; 23:43). It indicates the opportunity of salvation here and now. Furthermore, the use of the perfect indicative of a stative verb "has been fulfilled" (πεπλήρωται) in the clause stresses completed action in past time with continuing effect in the present.[48] What was foretold by Isaiah is being fulfilled in their midst by the implied agent, Jesus.[49] Green asserts that the prepositional phrase, "in your hearing" (ἐν τοῖς ὠσὶν ὑμῶν) not only invites, but also demands a response from the audience.[50]

---

46. Nolland, *Luke 1–9:20*, 198. Also, Bock says that this omission represents part of the "already-not-yet" tension of NT eschatology, and a Gospel writer can discuss an issue from either side of the temporal perspective. See Bock, *Luke 1:1–9:50*, 411.

47. Nolland, *Luke 1–9:20*, 198.

48. Fanning, *Verbal Aspect*, 292.

49. Culy, Parsons, and Stigall, *Luke*, 135.

50. Green, *Gospel of Luke*, 214.

## The Empowered Prophet Mighty in Words

> And all bore witness to him and were amazed at the words of grace coming from his mouth. Then they said, "Is this not the son of Joseph?" (4:22)

Luke now tells of how the people responded to the exposition of Jesus. Interestingly, all the verbs in this verse (v. 22) are in the imperfect tense. They can be classified as progressive (descriptive) imperfect, which according to Daniel B. Wallace describes an action or state that is in progress in past time from the viewpoint of the speaker.[51] In addition, when the progressive imperfect is used instead of an aorist, the imperfect highlights the manner of the occurrence while the aorist merely relates the fact of it.[52] This suggests that the sermon was riveting from the beginning to the end. Also, it describes the attitude of the people during the sermon. The people all "bore witness" (ἐμαρτύρουν) to his advantage or praised him (spoke well of).[53]

What startled the people was not his winsome eloquence, but "the words of grace" (τοῖς λόγοις τῆς χάριτος) coming from his mouth. It is not words about grace (objective genitive), but words characterized by grace (descriptive genitive).[54] More so, the locative dative with the preposition "at" (ἐπὶ) points to the words of grace as the reason why the people were astonished.[55] Nolland conveys the meaning well, he says that "grace" (χάρις) is the divine influence that is present in the words and that gives the words their quite tangible impact.[56] Jesus is the anointed prophet, mighty in words. The response of

---

51. Wallace, *Greek Grammar Beyond*, 543.

52. Fanning, *Verbal Aspect*, 243.

53. The phrase, "all bore witness to him" (πάντες ἐμαρτύρουν αὐτῷ), can be taken in the sense "to praise," with a dative of advantage (Acts 13:22; 14:3; 15:8; 22:5; Gal 4:15; Col 4:13), or in the sense "to bear witness against," i.e. "to condemn" (Matt 23:31; John 7:7). The former meaning is adopted here by most commentators. See Marshall, *Gospel of Luke*, 185.

54. Porter, *Idioms of the Greek*, 93.

55. Porter, 161.

56. Nolland, *Luke 1–9:20*, 199; Also, in his article, "Words of Grace," Nolland established the Lukan meaning of χάρις based on the use of the word in Luke's writing. He says Luke is saying that "it is precisely because Jesus's words are τῆς χάριτος that they have their impact. The people admit to the impact of the words on them; Luke wants his readers to see that it is the τῆς χάριτος, which makes it possible for the words to have their impact." See Nolland, "Words of Grace," 48; Garland concurs with Nolland but adds that the words can confer grace only if one listens in obedience. See Garland, *Luke*, 202. Frederic Louis Godet believes that "the words, which proceeded forth out of his mouth, express the fullness with which this proclamation poured forth from his heart." See Godet, *Commentary on Luke*, 151.

the people is at first favorable, but then there is a shift in mood. They ask, "Is this not the son of Joseph?" This is a sign of skepticism about his claim. The query is raised because of his interpretation of the Scripture and subsequent proclamation. The question reveals their disbelief. They were not ready to accept the word of the "son of Joseph" as the word of the anointed Son of God.[57]

## The Empowered Prophet Mighty in Works

> And he said to them, "Certainly you will say to me this proverb, 'Physician, heal yourself; what we have heard happened in Capernaum, do also here in your hometown.' And truly I say to you, no prophet is accepted in his hometown. But truly I say to you, many widows were in Israel in the days of Elijah, when the heavens were closed for three years and six months, as it happened a great famine upon all the land, and to none of them was Elijah sent except to Zarephath of Sidon to a widow woman. And there were many lepers in Israel in the time of Elisha the prophet, and none of them were cleansed except Naaman the Syrian." (4:23–27)

The gracious words were now turned into words of indictment of unbelief. Luke used the future tense, "you will say to me" (ἐρεῖτέ μοι) in verse 23, to indicate that Jesus was fully aware of their thoughts or intuition. It is an omniscience that surfaces repeatedly in the Lukan narrative (5:21–22; 6:7–8; 7:36–50; 9:47); it is one of the characteristics of a Spirit-empowered prophet. He, as a prophet, read their collective minds and cited a proverb, "Physician, heal yourself" (Ἰατρέ, θεράπευσον σεαυτόν). This proverb has several parallels.[58] Thus, Jesus was using this proverb to give a counter response to their demands for him to authenticate his credentials as the Messiah. Sloan writes, "Their offended and offensive reaction to Jesus evokes a counter response from him, which, in the face of their already manifested unbelief, predicted that they would next be demanding further proof of his messianic credentials,

---

57. Tiede, *Luke*, 109.

58. The proverb is found in different ancient literature with varying nuances. In Greek literature, one finds, "A Physician for others, but himself teeming with sores"; in later rabbinical literature, "Physician, heal your own lameness." See Fitzmyer, *According to Luke I–IX*, 535.

i.e., miracles."⁵⁹ The cynicism of the proverb is explained in the request to do what he did at Capernaum in Nazareth as well. The requests for mighty works or miracles started with the devil in 4:3 and will linger throughout the ministry of Jesus (11:16; 22:64; 23:8, 35–37). Implicitly, one can see that apart from the gracious words of Jesus, the people ascribed mighty works to him as well. Otherwise, they would not have asked him to do what he did in Capernaum.

Jesus, on the other hand, presents a rebuke to their desire for mighty works in verse 24. The rebuke is very strong because it is introduced by the asseverative particle, "Truly I say to you" or "Amen" (Ἀμὴν λέγω ὑμῖν), which is found either singularly or doubly over seventy times in the Gospels and only from the lips of Jesus for a solemn declaration.⁶⁰ Traditionally in Judaism, it is used at the end of a statement in order to authenticate what has been said, but Jesus used it to introduce and stress what follows.⁶¹ He says, "No prophet is accepted in his hometown."

Again, Jesus used another asseveration, "Truly" (ἀληθείας), to stress the validity of the comparison to follow. He employed two Old Testament stories involving Elijah and Elisha (cf. 1 Kgs 17:1–24; 2 Kgs 5:1–19). In both cases the two stories emphasize that there were many in Israel who would have benefited from the prophets; unfortunately, they did not, and only the Gentiles benefited. The Gentiles benefited from these prophets because they accepted them with joy. In fact, Luke would later show how, through his words and works, Jesus confirms to the disciples of John the Baptist that he is indeed the prophet to come, and that those who are not offended by this claim will be blessed (7:18–23). Ellis believes that the two stories emphasize the true meaning of the rejection at Nazareth: God will pass over a rebellious Israel and give his blessings to Gentiles.⁶² Undoubtedly, the Nazareth rejection provides a scriptural precedent for future preachers of the gospel. Tannehill holds that the rejection Jesus experienced at Nazareth will be experienced by

---

59. Sloan, *Favorable Year of the Lord*, 86. Others that hold this interpretation are Bock and Ellis.

60. BDAG, s.v. "Ἀμὴν." Rhetorically, the whole expression serves to introduce a statement of high importance (cf. 12:37; 18:17, 29; 21:32; 23:43). See Culy, Parsons, and Stigall, *Luke*, 137–38.

61. See Stein, *Luke*, 158; Ellis, *Gospel of Luke*, 98; Marshall, *Gospel of Luke*, 187.

62. Ellis, *Gospel of Luke*, 98.

his witnesses in Acts, leading them to turn from the Jews to Gentiles (Acts 13:44–47; 18:5–7; 28:24–28).[63]

## The Response of the People in Violent Rejection

> And all were filled with rage in the synagogue as they were hearing these things. And rising up they took him outside the city and led him to the edge of the hill upon which their city was built, in order to throw him down the cliff. But he went through their midst and went on his way. (4:28–30)

These verses describe the tragedy Jesus experienced among his people. Their mild unbelief has now turned to violent rejection. The impact of Jesus's words filled his audience with "rage" (θυμοῦ) as they were listening. Luke used a present participle, "hearing" (ἀκούοντες), to indicate that the crowd reacted while he was still teaching. He had not finished his sermon when they acted in indignation. What are the "these things" (ταῦτα) that aggravated the people in verse 28? The demonstrative pronoun ταῦτα is an accusative direct object of "hearing" (ἀκούοντες), referring to Jesus statements about the gentile mission and his Messianic claim in the previous verses. Marshall says it is the culmination of their resentment against a prophet whose words they failed to appreciate and who did nothing to justify his claim.[64]

Luke goes on to identify the crowd's intent in taking Jesus outside the city. He uses a purpose clause, "in order" (ὥστε), to spell out their intention, which was to throw him down the cliff. The infinitive verb, "to throw him down" (κατακρημνίσαι) is a hapax in the New Testament. Alessandro Falcetta in his famous work on this passage holds that Luke prefers to use a compound form κρημνίζω, which is the verb of crucifixion in Luke 23:39, Acts 5:30, and 10:39 because he is prefiguring the crucifixion of Christ.[65]

Luke does not explain why they were unable to kill Jesus; he says in verse 30, "he went through their midst" (διελθὼν διὰ μέσου αὐτῶν). The readers are left wondering how Jesus escaped from their hands, which has been debated. Ellis says it was because "his hour had not yet come" that Jesus was divinely

---

63. Tannehill, *Luke*, 94.
64. Marshall, *Gospel of Luke*, 190.
65. Falcetta, *Call of Nazareth*, 85.

protected from harm (cf. John 7:30, 45).⁶⁶ Consequently, Luke speaks of Jesus divinely led to proceed with his mission journey. Luke uses the verb "went on his way" (ἐπορεύετο), which he used often to make reference to the divine pattern laid out for the life of Jesus (cf. Luke 4:42; 7:6, 11; 9:51, 52, 53, 56, 57; 13:33; 17:11; 22:22).⁶⁷

## Theology of the Passage

The Nazareth episode is crucial to understanding the ministry of Jesus. Ray Summers believes that this incident is important because it reflects Jesus's understanding of his role as the Anointed One and the nature of the message he was sent to proclaim.⁶⁸ He goes on to say that it was this understanding and message that caused his hometown people to reject him and infuriated them to the point of attempting to kill him.⁶⁹ In sum, Bock writes:

> The synagogue incident of Luke 4:16–30 summarizes the nature of Jesus' ministry. Jesus is the Spirit-anointed prophet who announces the new era and brings to pass this salvation as the anointed Messiah (Isa. 61:1–2; 58:6). He is to proclaim the acceptable year of the Lord. He brings release to those held captive and to the needy. His own people demand that he display signs, yet they reject his claims. This is the first of many such rejections . . . In one pericope Jesus' ministry is outlined. Every reader faces a choice upon reading this account: to identify with Jesus and his message of hope or to side with those who reject Jesus.⁷⁰

Thus, the sermon in Nazareth teaches three theological truths: the mission of Jesus, the nature of his mission, and the result of his mission. It becomes the paradigm not only of Jesus's ministry but also the ministry of the church. Explicating these three theological truths is worth the quest of this research.

---

66. Ellis, *Gospel of Luke*, 98.
67. Nolland, *Luke 1–9:20*, 202; Bock, *Luke 1:1–9:50*, 420; Fitzmyer, *According to Luke I–IX*, 539; Green, *Gospel of Luke*, 219.
68. Summers, *Commentary on Luke*, 56.
69. Summers, 56.
70. Bock, *Luke 1:1–9:50*, 420.

First, the mission of Jesus is clearly seen from this passage in that the era of salvation has arrived, "Today this Scripture has been fulfilled in your hearing." The fulfillment of Scripture is to be found in the person and works of Jesus, who has been anointed with the Spirit and appears as the eschatological prophet – a figure who is to be identified with the Messiah and the servant of Yahweh.[71] According to Luke, Jesus came to seek and save the lost (Luke 19:10). Talbert in his article "The Lukan Presentation of Jesus' Ministry in Galilee" writes, "This ministry, according to Luke 4:16–30 is a fulfillment of the Old Testament (vv. 18–21). Though not referring exclusively to the Galilean ministry, the speeches of Acts also regard Jesus' ministry as a fulfillment of prophecy (3:22, 24; 10:43; 13:23, 27, 32, 40, etc.)."[72]

Second, the nature of the mission of Jesus is stated in the passage. One clause that captures the nature of Jesus's ministry is "to herald release to the captives" (κηρύξαι αἰχμαλώτοις ἄφεσιν). Green defines the Lukan understanding of "release" as wholeness, freedom from diabolic and social chains, which leads to acceptance.[73] The anointed Isaianic figure heralds and brings about salvation (deliverance). Jubilee release is an image of this salvation. This release encompasses spiritual restoration, moral transformation, rescue from demonic oppression, and release from illness and disability.[74]

This release is accomplished through the Spirit-empowered preaching of the good news with mighty words and the performance of mighty works (Spirit-work). It is through the words of Jesus that forgiveness, deliverance, and restoration come to reality. Jesus's words and works signal that he is the anointed prophet of God sent to bring about total emancipation. Nolland says, "As a charismatic figure, Jesus speaks words endued with the power of God's grace (v. 22). This grace guarantees the words a dramatic impact."[75] Undoubtedly, Luke throughout his Gospel presents Jesus as powerful orator and performer of mighty deeds, two aspects that are inextricably intertwined.[76]

---

71. Marshall, *Gospel of Luke*, 178.
72. Talbert, "Lukan Presentation," 491.
73. Green, *Theology of the Gospel*, 79.
74. Nolland, *Luke 1–9:20*, 202.
75. Nolland, 202.
76. Danker, *Luke*, 12. Furthermore, Danker holds that after Jesus, only Moses qualifies in Luke's twin-work for the accolade (word and deed). In Acts 7:22 Luke has Stephen repeat almost verbatim about Moses (terms reversed, and plural instead of singular) the formula uttered by Cleopas, "And he was powerful in his words and deeds." Both Jesus and Moses are

Finally, the narrative indicates the results of Jesus's sermon – that is, how the Spirit-empowered words of grace spoken by Jesus encountered rejection from his own native people. Luke testifies that the people all "bore witness" (ἐμαρτύρουν) to his advantage or praised him (or spoke well) initially, but they voluntarily found objection when they asked, "Is this not the son of Joseph?" On the grounds of their objection, Jesus pronounces the prophet's fate (i.e. rejection by those to whom he is sent). Just like many Israelites did not benefit from the ministries of Elijah and Elisha, so too the people in Nazareth will not benefit since they have chosen by their unbelief to be outsiders to what God is presently doing.[77] It should be noted that Luke in the subsequent passages speaks of Jesus's acceptance by tax collectors, sinners, and the poor,[78] implying that the mission of Jesus and the church will either be rejected or accepted.

Furthermore, the Nazareth manifesto depicts the inclusion of the Gentiles (2:30–32; 3:6) in God's plan of salvation. Jesus used the illustrations of Elijah and Elisha to underscore the fact that God does not show partiality. Fitzmyer sees these illustrations as a justification from the Old Testament for the Christian mission to the Gentiles.[79] The overarching picture is that God desires to save all, not only the chosen race of Israel. It is a global rescue plan that God has embarked upon through the Messiah. Garland writes:

> He [Jesus] seeks to insert a wide-angle lens on their perspective of the world so that they will focus on more than their narrow self-interest. He does more than speak gracious words, but by his words and his ensuing actions, he intends to give them a vision so that they can get beyond wanting God to do something

---

benefactors par excellence, but Jesus causes an "exodus" that supersedes Moses' accomplishment. See Danker, 12.

77. Nolland, *Luke 1–9:20*, 203.

78. Talbert asserts that there is both a rejection by his own people and a hint of a wider mission to all kinds of people (vv. 23–24, 25–27). Though the speeches of Acts refer only to Jesus's rejection in connection with Jerusalem, that the evangelist intended this rejection, as well as the wider circle of ministry, to apply also to Galilee, may be seen if we examine the introduction to the second part of the Galilean section, namely, 7:18–30. Here not only is Jesus's ministry of healing and preaching a fulfillment of Old Testament prophecy, but also, though it is met with rejection by the Jewish leaders, it finds acceptance among the people and the tax collectors (vv. 29–30). See Talbert, "Lukan Presentation," 491.

79. Fitzmyer, *According to Luke I–IX*, 537.

only for themselves and see what God is doing for the world through him.[80]

The empowerment of the Holy Spirit leads to effective preaching with words of grace that brings about release for all people in the world who would acknowledge their need and respond appropriately.

## Conclusion: Implications for Preaching

O'Reilly affirms that the type of ministry envisaged by Luke's use of Isaiah 61 in 4:18 is clearly a prophetic one, a ministry of powerful preaching and mighty works.[81] Jesus publicly testified in this passage that the nature of his empowerment was demonstrated in his words and works. At his baptism, he was empowered with the Spirit as a prophet with a task. This empowerment was to enable him to inaugurate the era of salvation through his powerful preaching. Jesus was equipped by the Spirit to be mighty in words and deeds. In sum, Jesus was mighty in words and deeds because God empowered him with the power of the Spirit. John the Baptist was right when he said, "A man can receive nothing unless it has been given him from heaven" (John 3:27 NKJV).

---

80. Garland, *Luke*, 210. It should also be noted that many scholars have written extensively about the Jew-Gentile mission in Luke. Larrimore C. Crockett sees a fellowship between Jews and Gentiles when he asserts that

> Luke 4:25–27 must be seen as a prolepsis not simply of the Gentile mission, and certainly not of God's rejection of Israel and turning to the Gentiles, but rather of Jewish-Gentile *reconciliation*, the *cleansing* of the Gentiles, which makes it possible for Jews and Gentiles to live and eat together in the new age. Since these verses are set in the context of Jesus' rejection at Nazareth, our interpretation of them obviously raises questions about the meaning of the Nazareth pericope as a whole. The insight into Luke's use of Elijah-widow and Elisha-Naaman as models for Jewish-Gentile relations leads, in my opinion, to a revision of the usual interpretation of the Nazareth pericope and ultimately to a re-assessment of Luke's use of the OT in Luke-Acts. As I have shown elsewhere, such a reassessment reveals that Luke's use of the OT was dominated by the Jewish-Gentile question, and his resolution of the problem strives toward the view that *despite* what happened at Nazareth, and in a marvelous way *because* of what happened there (which reaches its climax in the crucifixion), the destiny of both Jews and Gentiles is bound up with Jesus Christ, and it is God's intention, through him, to save and heal both, together.

See Crockett, "Luke 4:25–27," 183; Craig A. Evans see the Elijah/Elisha narratives in Luke as a teaching on election. He says, the Elijah/Elisha references and allusions are clearest, the theme of election or ecclesiology is present if not paramount. See Evans and Sanders, *Luke and Scripture*, 82.

81. O'Reilly, *Word and Sign*, 31.

If the empowerment of the Spirit is a gift, characterized by mighty words and works, then it implies that there are criteria for empowerment. These criteria are not divinely endowed without human responsibility.

First, God only empowers those preachers whom he has sent. As seen previously (in chapter 1), Ricoeur believes that a witness is not just anyone who comes forward and gives testimony, but the one who is sent to testify.[82] Jesus was a prophet sent by God. He was sent to proclaim good news to the poor. Luke would later portray Jesus (the sent one) as the sending one. Luke says, "And He called the twelve together, and gave them power and authority over all the demons and to heal diseases. And He sent them out to proclaim the kingdom of God and to perform healing" (9:1–2 NASB). Like Jesus, the disciples were empowered and sent to preach. A preacher is sent to preach (Rom 10:13–15). Although all Christians are confessional witnesses, it should be noted that preaching is a different kind of witnessing. Lloyd-Jones says, "Every Christian should be able to give an account of why he is a Christian; but that does not mean that every Christian is meant to preach."[83] There is an empowerment for preaching, which God gives to those whom he calls. Every preacher needs to ask himself whether he has been called or not. Also, all those who are called need to respond like Isaiah, who said to the Lord when he was called, "Here am I. Send me" (Isa 6:8 NASB).

Second, absolute surrender to the Spirit's leading is essential for empowerment. Notice how Luke describes the Spirit in the life of Jesus in Luke 4. He says, "Jesus, full of the Holy Spirit, returned from the Jordan and was led around by the Spirit in the wilderness" (4:1 NASB). After the temptation in the wilderness, Luke says, "And Jesus returned to Galilee in the power of the Spirit, and news about Him spread through all the surrounding district" (4:14 NASB). The Spirit led Jesus into the wilderness, and the Spirit led him into Galilee. Beyond chapter 4, Luke emphasizes the role of the Holy Spirit

---

82. Ricoeur, "Hermeneutics of Testimony," 131.

83. Lloyd-Jones, *Preaching and Preachers*, 102. Stephen F. Olford and David L. Olford believe that all Christians are "called ones." This basic "call" is to Christ as Lord and savior (Eph 1:18; 4:1; 2; 2 Tim 1:9; Heb 3:1; 2 Pet 1:10). But God also calls with a view to "good works, which God prepared in advance for us to do" (Eph 2:10). Included in the "good works" is the call to preach. The call of Moses (Exod 3:4–22), of Samuel (1 Sam 3:4), of Jeremiah (Jer 1:4–10), and in New Testament, the call of the disciples (Mark 3:13–19), of Paul (Rom 1:1; 1 Cor 1:1; Gal 1:15), and of Barnabas (Acts 13:2) are all good examples. See Olford and Olford, *Anointed Expository Preaching*, 7–8.

frequently in the life and ministry of Jesus. Jesus of Nazareth, a man Spirit conceived (1:35) and Spirit confirmed/anointed (3:22), a man proclaiming his message through the Spirit (4:18; 10:21; 11:20; Acts 1:2), and after his resurrection he mediates the Spirit to his followers (24:49; Acts 2:33).[84] Jesus's entire life revolves around the prompting of the Spirit. Absolute surrender to the leading of the Holy Spirit is crucial if a preacher is to experience the empowerment of the Spirit in preaching.

Third, spiritual disciplines are the means through which the empowerment of the Spirit remains active. Donald S. Whitney defines spiritual disciplines as "those personal and corporate disciplines that promote spiritual growth. They are the habits of devotion and experiential Christianity that have been practiced by the people of God since biblical times."[85] Immediately after his empowerment, Jesus was led by the Spirit into the wilderness to fast for forty days (4:1–2). In addition, Luke goes on to stress Jesus's habitual frequenting of the synagogue; he says, "And he entered the synagogue according to his custom on the Sabbath day" (4:16). In fact, Luke was the only evangelist to narrate the incident where Jesus's parents left the Passover feast without him when he was twelve years old. After three days, his parents found him in the temple at Jerusalem; he was sitting in the midst of teachers, hearing them and asking questions. He was upset that they came looking for him and he said to them, "Why is it that you were looking for me? Did you not know that I had to be in my Father's house?" (2:49). He loved attending the temple worship. Jesus was also a man of prayer (5:16; 6:12; 11:1). In sum, he was a man of unbroken piety. The apostles and disciples in the book of Acts emulated this pietistic lifestyle. Without constant communion with God, a preacher is powerless! John Piper says, "The aroma of God will not linger on a person who does not linger in the presence of God."[86]

---

84. Ellis, *Gospel of Luke*, 10. Also, Ellis says that "witness" in the Gospel is the witness of the Spirit, most often through the acts and teachings of Jesus (Luke 4:31–22: 53) but also through Old Testament and contemporary prophets (1:5–2: 40; 3:16). The Spirit is the same Spirit of the Lord who spoke through the prophets (4:18; Acts 1:16), but he now appears in a new role. This role determines the meaning of Jesus's messiahship and of his message of the kingdom of God. What the Spirit foretold through the prophets he now accomplished through Messiah. See Ellis, 10.

85. Whitney, *Spiritual Disciplines*, 17. Whitney goes on to examine the various spiritual disciplines in the Scripture: Bible intake, prayer, worship, evangelism, service, stewardship, fasting, silence and solitude, journaling, and learning. See Whitney, 17.

86. Piper, *Supremacy of God*, 63.

Finally, God empowers those who submit to the authority of Scripture and who commit themselves to its exposition. By exposition, we affirm Walter L. Liefeld's simple definition of expository preaching as explanation applied.[87] The goal or essence of exposition is application. Luke says, Jesus "sat down" (ἐκάθισεν) to give exposition of the Isaiah passage; he submitted himself to biblical authority. Jesus knew that he was the climax of God's revelation to man, yet he was also aware that the spoken word of God through Isaiah had a binding force for all succeeding generations. J. I. Packer says, "God's historical utterances thus operate like statute law in society. Enactments of various dates, once on the statute book, remain continually in force, applying in principles to everyone . . . and each generation is obliged to comply with what 'the laws say.'"[88] A preacher who submits to biblical exposition, explicitly affirms that God speaks through the written word. It is through submission to biblical authority that one's words become "words of grace" as was obvious in Jesus's sermon in Nazareth.

---

87. Liefeld, *New Testament Exposition*, 6.
88. Packer, *God Has Spoken*, 78.

CHAPTER 3

# Two Disciples' Testimony about Jesus: Luke 24:13–35

The previous chapter established the testimony of Jesus about himself as one empowered with the Holy Spirit to fulfill his messianic task. Jesus affirmed that Spirit empowerment is demonstrated in mighty words and mighty works. In this chapter, the testimony of two disciples about Jesus in Luke 24:13–35 will be analyzed exegetically as well. The goal is similar to the previous chapter and is threefold: (1) to establish the testimony of two disciples about the identity of Jesus as a prophet mighty in words and works; (2) to validate the claim that Spirit-empowered witnessing is demonstrated by mighty words and works; and (3) to assess the implications of the passage to preaching.

## Historical Context

Some assumptions regarding the Gospel of Luke were made in the preceding chapter, and the historical context was discussed. Also, the literary structure of the Gospel of Luke was affirmed as well. Consequently, this chapter will not revisit questions on historical background that have been previously discussed; rather, it will build upon it. Suffice it to say that just like the Nazareth sermon in Luke 4, which has no parallel in the Gospels, the same can be said of the testimony of the two disciples walking to Emmaus. What is the source of this account? Extensive scholarly discussion of the Lukan source(s) has been proposed. Bock summarized the three main views canvassed: (1) the material came directly from one of the travelers; (2) Luke received the basic story from a source, although there is disagreement about which elements came from this source; and (3) the material is basically Luke's, from his hand, and with his emphases.[1] It is difficult to determine the source(s) of this account. In fact, Tiede noted that it is futile to attempt to identify Luke's source(s) or to separate the verses into possible pre-Lukan documents.[2] In light of this difficulty, we concur with the assertion of Marshall that "we are justified in regarding this story as having a basis in historical tradition, and that the hand of Luke in the formation of the narrative cannot be denied, but he was by no means creating his story *de novo*."[3]

## Literary Context

Luke 24 is the account of the resurrection of Jesus. It is composed of three major scenes, the empty tomb (24:1–12), the journey to Emmaus (24:13–35), and farewell with final commission (24:36–53). According to Marshall, the main purpose of the story is to guarantee the fact of the resurrection (cf. Acts 1:3) by emphasizing (1) that it is the expected fulfillment of the Old Testament, and (2) that the risen Lord appeared to witnesses and was recognized to be Jesus.[4] Furthermore, Luke was seeking to affirm his accurate description of Jesus from the perspective of the disciples. Tannehill writes, "The description of Jesus in v. 19 as a 'prophet powerful in work and word before God and all the people' is not an indication of ignorance but reflects a view of Jesus characteristic of Luke-Acts, being expressed both by authoritative characters and by the narrator."[5]

In terms of structure, Ellis holds that the three resurrection episodes are dovetailed into one another; the empty tomb account (24:1–12) is virtually repeated in the Emmaus story (24:22–24), and the Emmaus teaching (24:25–27) is reiterated in the following scene (24:44–49).[6] Furthermore, the journey to Emmaus is connected to the previous episode by noting that they both occurred on the same first day of the week. Some scholars see a chiastic pattern:

---

1. Bock, *Luke 9:51–24:53*, 1904.
2. Tiede, *Luke*, 433.
3. Marshall, *Gospel of Luke*, 891.
4. Marshall, 891.
5. Tannehill, *Narrative Unity*, 280.
6. Ellis, *Gospel of Luke*, 271.

A Journey from Jerusalem (24:13–14)
  B Closed eyes (24:15–17)
    C Explanation without understanding (24:18–24)
      D Suffering and glory (24:25–26)
    C' Explanation with understanding (24:27)
  B' Opened eyes (24:28–32)
A' Return to Jerusalem (24:33–35).[7]

From the chiastic structure above, it is obvious that the linchpin of this passage is in sections C, D, and C'. This analysis will take A and B together as the introduction (vv. 13–17), section C will be considered as the testimony of two disciples about Jesus's identity (vv. 18–24). Next, D and C' will be taken together as the exposition of the prophet mighty in words and works (vv. 25–27). Finally, B' and A' will be examined together as the result of the exposition of the prophet mighty in words and works (vv. 28–35).

## Exegesis of Luke 24:13–35

Before proceeding with exegetical analysis, it is important to establish the text critically. According to UBS[5], there are six textual variants in this pericope. Of the six, three were designated {B} by the committee; however, they do not affect the meaning of the text.[8] Two variants were not given a designation by Metzger but are important to note. The first is in 24:18: codex S and V added the identity of the other person traveling with "Cleopas" (Κλεοπᾶς). Codex S (which dates from AD 949) adds in the margin that the one traveling with Cleopas was Simon, not Peter but the other (Simon), while codex V (which

---

7. Garland, *Luke*, 949. Also see Green, *Gospel of Luke*, 842.

8. The first variant is in 24:13, the word "sixty" (ἑξήκοντα). The variant reading has (ἑκατον ἑξήκοντα), which have arisen in connection with patristic identification of Emmaus with "Amwas," about twenty-two Roman miles (176 stadia) from Jerusalem. Metzger asserts that it is too far for the travelers to have re-traversed that same evening (v. 33), therefore, the "seven" added is undoubtedly due to a scribal blunder. The second variant is in 24:17, the word, "they stood" (ἐστάθησαν). According to Metzger, the committee preferred ἐστάθησαν rather than ἐστε, which is supported by most other witnesses. And the third variant with the {B} designation is in 24:19, the word "Nazareth" (Ναζαρηνοῦ). Metzger says, "It is probable that scribes replaced the less frequently used word Ναζαρηνος (six times in the New Testament, including one other time in Luke [nowhere in Acts]) by the more frequently used Ναζωραῖος (thirteen times in the New Testament, including eight times in Luke and Acts)." See Metzger, *Textual Commentary*, 158–59.

dates from the ninth century) has a marginal note that asserts that the one with Cleopas was Nathanael.[9] The second undesignated variant reading is in 24:32, the word, "burning" (καιομένη). The word seems to have troubled many copyists. According to Metzger, some copyist translated the word as "veiled," while others used "blinded" or "hardened," however, the translation as "burning," attested by the overwhelming preponderance of witnesses, best suits the context.[10] Therefore, we will use the word "burning."

Finally, the sixth variant is in 24:32, which is given a {C} designation. The shorter reading, which reads, "as he spoke to us" (ὡς ἐλάλει ἡμῖν) was adopted by the primary Alexandrian witnesses, however, the committee preferred the longer reading "within us as he spoke to us" ([ἐν ἡμῖν] ὡς ἐλάλει ἡμῖν). The hesitancy by the committee to omit the prepositional phrase "within us" (ἐν ἡμῖν) is due to the possibility that a copyist may have deleted them as superfluous in the context.[11] I will adopt the longer reading in this work. Thus, with the text established, what follows is the exegetical work.

## The Introduction to the Narrative

> And behold, on that same day, two of them were going to a village called Emmaus, about seven miles from Jerusalem, and they were conversing with each other about all the things that had happened. While they were talking and discussing, Jesus himself drew near and walked along with them, but their eyes were kept from recognizing him. And he said to them, "What is this conversation you are exchanging with each other as you walk?" And they stood still full of gloom. (24:13–17)

Luke begins this narrative by asserting that it occurred on the same day with the previous event (empty tomb); this implies that both events took place on the resurrection day (24:1). On that same day, "two of them" (δύο ἐξ αὐτῶν), which refers back to the group of the disciples mentioned in 24:9, went on a journey. These two disciples are not part of the apostles because Cleopas is not one of the twelve. Supposedly, they were among the group of the other

---

9. Metzger, 158.
10. Metzger, 159.
11. Metzger.

disciples besides the twelve that walked with Jesus. So, they were going to a village called Emmaus, about seven miles away. Their motivation for this journey was not given. However, Luke described their destination as being near Jerusalem. Although the location of Emmaus is still debated, Tiede proposed that Luke's point of mentioning Emmaus is to state that it was an extended walk on the road, yet close enough so that the disciples could return quickly to Jerusalem (v. 35).[12]

During this journey, the disciples were conversing with each other about all the things that had happened. While the pair was discussing, a third traveler (Jesus) drew near from the rear and began to walk along with them. Luke makes it clear that the two disciples were "kept" (ἐκρατοῦντο) from recognizing Jesus. The passive verb implies that the agent of the restraining action was God, the divine passive. It is not clear why God concealed their eyes. Contextually, one may assert that it was done to avoid distraction during Jesus's exposition of Scriptures to the disciples (vv. 25–27).

So, Jesus joined the conversation by asking about the words they were exchanging with each other. The verb "exchange" (ἀντιβάλλετε) is a New Testament *hapax legomenon*, which denotes a winsome imagery of conversation. A. T. Robertson said the Greek word ἀντιβάλλετε carries the idea of throwing back and forth like a ball, from one to another, which is a beautiful picture of conversation as a game of words.[13] In a nutshell, Jesus was asking them to repeat the substance of their conversation, in order that he might join in the game. It was depressing to them, so they stood still. Luke used an adjective of manner, "full of gloom" (σκυθρωποί) to describe their grief. They were not grieved with him wanting to join their conversation, but the topic of their conversation was a lament. And they were perplexed because they assumed that everyone ought to be talking about the recent event.[14]

---

12. Tiede, *Luke*, 434. Bock has a different view: he holds a twofold significance of Emmaus: (1) it indicates an appearance in the Jerusalem area, which is Luke's geographic concern, and (2) it reflects the retention of historical details. It is hard to imagine an appearance being tied to an obscure village unless it really occurred there. Luke thus sets the stage for one of the most famous of Jesus's appearances. See Bock, *Luke 9:51–24:53*, 1908–9.

13. Robertson, *Word Pictures*, 180.

14. Bock says, "Their reaction to Jesus' question is simple: they stop walking ... They cannot believe that anyone coming out of Jerusalem does not know what has happened. Clearly these travelers are stunned and disappointed by recent events." See Bock, *Luke 9:51–24:53*, 1910.

## The Testimony of the Two Disciples About Jesus's Ministry

> Then one of them, named Cleopas, answered him, "Are you the only stranger in Jerusalem who does not know the things that have happened there in these days?" And he said to them, "what things?" And they said to him, "things concerning Jesus of Nazareth, who was a prophet mighty in work and word before God and all the people, and how our chief priests and leaders handed him over to be sentenced to death and had him crucified. But we had hoped that he would be the one to redeem Israel. And indeed, besides all this, it is the third day since these things happened. But also, some women of our group astonished us; they went to the tomb early this morning, and not finding his body they came back to report that they had even seen a vision of angels, who told them that he was alive. And some of those with us went to the tomb and found it just as the women had said, but they did not see him." (vv. 18–24)

Jesus receives a response from one of the disciples, named Cleopas. Fitzmyer noted that Cleopas is the shortened form of the Greek name Kleopatros, the masculine form of Cleopatra.[15] Nowhere in the New Testament is Cleopas identified. Cleopas and his companion were shocked at the ignorance of Jesus. They asked, "Are you the only stranger in Jerusalem who does not know the things that have happened there in these days?" It implies that what happened to Jesus of Nazareth was not a secret event. It was a public event known by all in Jerusalem. Jesus asked them, "What things?" This further prompting by Jesus will lead the two disciples to confess their testimony about Jesus of Nazareth. Also, both disciples were involved in the speech that follows, although Cleopas appears to be the leader.

The disciples said to him, "The things concerning Jesus of Nazareth" (v. 19). They then stated their thoughts about Jesus of Nazareth. First, the two disciples affirmed Jesus as a prophet from Nazareth mighty in work and word. Luke used a relative clause that functions adjectivally to make further assertion that Jesus of Nazareth was a prophet. The two disciples made this assertion in verse 19, although Luke had already echoed the identity of Jesus

---

15. Fitzmyer, *According to Luke X–XXIV*, 1563.

as a prophet (4:24; 7:16; 9:19; and 13:33). The title "prophet" was not descriptive enough for the disciples, and so an attributive modifier was added to give a vivid picture of Jesus's prophetic credentials. Literally, "Jesus was a man, a prophet, one who was powerful in deed and word." Besides Acts 1:1, all the summaries of the ministry of Jesus in Acts either speak of his teaching (4:18–19, 44; 8:1; 15:1; 19:47; 20:1; 21:37), or work (2:22; 10:38; 4:40–41; 13:32); but in this clause, Luke combines the two together with a conjunction (ἔργῳ καὶ λόγῳ). These two marks (work and word) are complementary and distinguished Jesus as a prophet. Richard J. Dillon writes,

> The δυναμίς of his deeds and words was the fruit of his "Spirit" endowment (Lk 3,22; 4,1), and this was programmatic of Lk's account of the public ministry . . . The same pattern of presentation and accreditation applied to the messiah's followers in the worldwide mission (Lk 9,1; 24:49; Acts 1:8; 3,12; 4,7–33 [the twelve]; 6:8 [Stephen]; 8:13 [Philip]; 19,11–12 [Paul]). Moreover, corresponding to the articulation of the messianic ministry in powerful "deed and word" (Lk 24:19; Acts 1:1) is the combination of wondrous things "seen and heard" as credentials of the Lord's witnesses (Lk 7:22; 10:24; Acts 4:20; cp. Acts 22,15; 2,33).[16]

Undoubtedly, Spirit-empowered witnessing is not a separation of work and word, but a combination of both as seen above.

Furthermore, the disciples affirmed that Jesus was a prophet par excellence like Moses, who was mighty in words and deeds. The two disciples' words are echoed almost exactly in Stephen's eulogy of Moses in Acts 7:22, where Stephen argued that as Moses's mission encountered rejection by the Israelites, so also was Jesus's mission opposed by the leaders (Acts 7:35–37).[17] This authenticates that Jesus was the future prophet Moses spoke about in Deuteronomy 18:15. But the travelers did not rest only in Moses's prediction of Jesus as a prophet. They also pointed to God and their people's opinion as indicated in the prepositional phrase, "Before God and all the people" (ἐναντίον τοῦ θεοῦ καὶ παντὸς τοῦ λαοῦ). This phrase evokes the imagery of a

---

16. Dillon, *From Eye-Witnesses*, 114–15.
17. Dillon, 122.

courtroom, where verdicts are passed in the sight or judgment of others.[18] This implies that the description of Jesus as a prophet mighty in works and words is an opinion held also by God and the people (4:15; 7:29; 18:43; 19:48; 21:38).

Second, the two disciples affirmed Jesus's rejection and death by crucifixion in verse 20. The disciples believe that their chief priests and leaders were responsible for the death of Jesus. Fitzmyer says, "Thus at the end of the Gospel Luke makes one of the subordinate characters point his finger again directly at the Jewish authorities as responsible for the death of Jesus, without any mention of Pilate or the Romans."[19] The verb "handed over" (παρέδωκαν) alludes to the passive role of the Romans in the crucifixion of Jesus.[20]

Third, the two disciples expressed in verse 21 the despondency that came over their group as a result of Jesus's death. Their hope was that Jesus (like Moses) would fulfill his prophetic work by liberating them from the oppression of the Romans. This is implied by the complementary infinitive, "to redeem" (λυτροῦσθα). The word "redeem" (λυτροω) here makes reference to a redeemer not to a ransom.[21] The awaited redemption (λυτρωσις) of Israel (Luke 1:68; and 2:38) from the yoke of their enemies as in Luke 1:71 was to come through the Messiah. Unfortunately, this is now the third day since their hope had been taken away. Tiede writes, "The key sentence in v. 21, therefore, is both a lament of our failed hopes of Israel's redemption and a confession of faithlessness."[22]

Last, the disciples revealed their skepticism about the resurrection in verses 22–24. Luke used an adversative conjunction "but" (ἀλλά) to introduce a clause that runs counter to expectation, implying that what the disciples have

---

18. BDAG, s.v. "ἐναντίον."

19. Fitzmyer, *According to Luke X–XXIV*, 1564.

20. Marshall, *Gospel of Luke*, 895; Bock, *Luke 9:51–24:53*, 1913.

21. TDNT, s.v. "λυτρωσις." Also, BDAG, s.v. "λυτρωσις." In addition, Dillon holds that the expression λυτροῦσθαι τὸν Ἰσραήλ (cf. Luke 1:68; 2:38) rejoins the Mosaic typology of v. 19, as a glance at Acts 7:35 will establish. For one thing, one cannot fail to notice the structural similarity between Stephen's statement about the rejected Moses and the kerygmatic declarations of God's vindication of the Messiah who was put to death (Acts 2:36; 5:30). Moreover, the same statement stands in a sequence (7:35–37) containing crucial elements we have noted in our present passage: prophet-title, wondrous works, public repudiation. Whether or not Luke also infused these elements into the martyr's speech, the remarkable parallelism of the passage elucidates the one at hand. Jesus and Moses, precisely as mighty prophets rejected, are the two historic "deliverers" of God's people. See Dillon, *From Eye-Witnesses*, 131–32.

22. Tiede, *Luke*, 435.

said remains valid in their opinion despite the latest report they are about to state. Neither the report of the empty tomb nor the story of an angelic vision was enough to convince them of the resurrection (vv. 22–24). According to Marshall, the reports by the women and some members of their group only heighten the tragedy.[23] In fact, in verse 24, the last clause, αὐτὸν δὲ οὐκ εἶδον, clearly emphasizes their skepticism. The pronoun "him" (αὐτὸν), is fronted in the clause for prominence; literally, "but him they did not see." This skepticism and unbelief are clearly stated in Tiede's words:

> The irony, however, is now more poignant as these two "witnesses" report to Jesus, whom they do not recognize, that the women "did not see" Jesus (also Peter in 24:12). Amazement, wonder, and disbelief are not the same as mockery and unbelief, but they are filled with their own pathos. The tension is high in the narrative, because Jesus and the reader can see and understand.[24]

The two disciples were correct about the prophetic identity of Jesus of Nazareth, whom they affirmed as mighty in works and words; however, they were skeptical about the report of his resurrection. It took the risen Christ himself in the next section to correct their unbelief.

## The Exposition of the Prophet Mighty in Words and Works

> And he said to them, "O you foolish and slow of heart to believe all that the prophets have spoken. Was it not necessary for the Christ to suffer all these things before entering into his glory?" And beginning from Moses and from all the prophets, he interpreted for them in all the Scriptures things concerning himself. (vv. 25–27)

After hearing their testimony, Jesus responded with a rebuke. The rebuke was expressed with a deep emotional (exasperation) disappointment by the

---

23. Marshall, *Gospel of Luke*, 896. Fitzmyer said, "The report of the women, who first noted the empty tomb, brings not credence, but astonishment, incredulous astonishment." See Fitzmyer, *According to Luke X–XXIV*, 1565.

24. Tiede, *Luke*, 435–36.

use of the vocative particle, "O" (Ὦ).²⁵ Maximilian Zerwick writes, "This is but a little particle, but it casts such a light on the state of mind of our Lord and of his apostles, that no one, surely, in reading the Scriptures, would wish to neglect its indications."²⁶ Jesus attributed their unbelief to the attitude of their heart, which in this case was described as foolish and slow. If they had believed all that the prophets have said about the Messiah, then they would have believed the women's report of the empty tomb. E. W. Bullinger writes, "This was the rebuke for Jewish disciples, but Christians today need it as much: for both believe and receive some Scriptures, but not 'All.'"²⁷ What follows in verses 26–27 is a condensed articulation of the kerygma from the Old Testament.

Jesus begins his exposition of the gospel with a rhetorical question. Was it not necessary for the Christ to suffer all these things before entering into his glory? The rhetorical interrogation begins with a negative particle, "not" (οὐχὶ), which indicates that a positive answer is expected to this question.²⁸ Jesus in verse 26 summarized the destiny of the Messiah in terms of suffering and entrance into glory. The imperfect verb ἔδει indicates that the suffering and entrance into glory were part of the divine will of God allotted for the Messiah.²⁹ The rest of Jesus's exposition of Scripture is given in a summary

---

25. The vocative particle ὦ is reserved for special use in the New Testament. It occurs in the beginning of a sentence where emotion is expressed (Matt 15:28; Luke 22:57; 24:25; Acts 3:10; Gal 3:1; 1 Tim 6:20; Jas 2:20). See Moulton, *Grammar of New Testament*, 33.

26. Zerwick, *Biblical Greek*, 36.

27. Bullinger, *Figures of Speech*, 930.

28. According to A. T. Robertson, if an affirmative or negative answer is expected, then that fact is shown by the use of οὐ for the question expecting the affirmative reply and by μή for the negative answer. See Robertson, *Grammar of the Greek*, 917.

29. TDNT, s.v. "δεῖ." Also, the term may be used as a general expression for the will of God, the statement with which it is linked thereby acquiring the significance of a rule of life (Luke 15:32; 18:1; Acts 5:29; 20:35). Jesus sees his whole life and ativity and passion under this will of God comprehended in a δεῖ. Over him there stands a δεῖ which is already present in his childhood. This is the δεῖ of the divine lordship (Luke 2:49). It determines his activity (Luke 4:43; 13:33; 19:5). It leads him to suffering and death, but also to glory (Luke 9:22; 17:25; 24:7, 26; Acts 1:16; 3:21; 17:3). It has its basis in the will of God concerning him that is laid down in Scripture and which he unconditionally follows (Luke 22:37; 24:44). His disiples, apostles, and community are also laid under this δεῖ, which derives from the will of God. Claimed by the divine will, they are shaped and determined by it down to the smallest details of their lives (Luke 12:12; Acts 9:6,16; 14:22; 19:21; 23:11; 27:24). Furthermore, the usage of Luke has the widest implications. It gathers up all the relations within which δεῖ is found in the rest of the New Testament. The word δεῖ expresses the necessity of the eschatological event, and is thus an eschatological term in the New Testament. It is well adapted for this role, since the eschatological

form. Luke does not cite any passage of Scripture in the exposition. Rather, Luke is fond of stressing that all Scripture points to Jesus (Luke 24:45; Acts 17:2, 11; 18:24, 28). He starts from Moses and goes through all the prophets, interpreting for them in all the Scriptures things concerning him. His point is to say that the risen Christ confronted the doubting disciples with Scripture. Fitzmyer holds that Christ's message to the two disciples is that from one end of the Hebrew Scriptures to the other they bear testimony about him and his fate, for Christ is the goal and center of all the Scriptures.[30]

## The Result of the Exposition of the Prophet Mighty in Words and Works

> And they drew near to the village where they were going, and he acted as though he were going farther. But they urged him strongly, saying "Remain with us, for it is near evening and the day is almost over." And he entered to remain with them. And it happened while he reclined at table with them, he took bread, blessed and broke it and gave it to them. Then their eyes were opened, and they recognized him; and he disappeared from them. They said to one another, "Were not our hearts burning within us as he spoke to us on the road, as he opened the Scripture?" And they rose up at that same hour and returned to Jerusalem and found the eleven gathered and those with them, and saying, "Truly the Lord has been raised and appeared to Simon." And they explained to them about the things that had happened to them in the breaking of bread. (vv. 28–35)

Luke brings his narrative to an interesting conclusion. At sunset, the two disciples reached their destination and Jesus acted as though he was going farther. He is giving them an opportunity to practice hospitality, which they did by urging him to remain with them. The risen Lord accepted their invitation to stay, and when they reclined for dinner he took the bread, blessed it, broke it, and gave it to them. The entire scenario of taking and breaking

---

event is one which is hidden from man, which can be known only by special revelation, and which sets man before an inconceivable necessity of historical occurence grounded in the divine will. See TDNT, s.v. "δεῖ."

30. Fitzmyer, *According to Luke X–XXIV*, 1567.

of the bread in verse 30 is reminiscent of the feeding of the five thousand in 9:16, and the last supper in 22:19. They were familiar with his action of blessing and breaking bread, but even then they were not able to recognize him because their eyes were kept from recognizing him, according to verse 16. Dillon writes, "Luke's travelers did not recognize the Master not because of his appearance [in another form – Mark 16:12] but because of the divinely determined economy of concealment and revelation whereby the truth of Christ's person and destiny was finally to be disclosed."[31]

Luke then used the conjunction δὲ in verse 31 to introduce the next significant episode. It was at that moment that their eyes were "opened" (διηνοίχθησαν) by God to recognize Jesus. They would later identify the meal as the defining moment of their experience with the risen Lord in verse 35. After they recognized him, Jesus disappeared. That was when they were able to verbalize the effect of the "opening" (διήνοιγεν) of the Scriptures on the road. They described it as "burning" (καιομένη) in their hearts. The word καίω means, "to burn" or "to kindle." It occurs thirteen times in the New Testament.[32] Of these instances, only its uses in this verse and 1 Corinthians 13:3 are theologically significant. The two disciples were employing a Jewish figurative expression of an emotional experience to describe the convincing effect of Jesus's exposition prior to his revelation.[33] According to Nolland, "The two disciples recalled that even before they recognized Jesus his interpretations of the Scriptures (24:27) were already at work convincing them of his resurrection."[34] Without any further delay, they returned to Jerusalem and rehearsed their experience with the risen Lord to the eleven disciples.

## Theology of the Passage

The journey to Emmaus was included in Luke's resurrection narrative accounts. The resurrection narrative started with the voices of the women of the empty tomb (24:1–12). Next, the testimony of the two disciples walking to Emmaus added to the voices of the women and Peter (24:13–35). Finally,

---

31. Dillon, *From Eye-Witnesses*, 146.
32. TDNT, s.v. "καίω."
33. BDAG, s.v. "καίω."
34. Nolland, *Luke 18:35–24:53*, 613.

the Lord appeared to the community of the disciples to validate all the voices and to commission them (24:36–53). There are three theological themes that can be deduced from the Emmaus account of the resurrection.

First, the Emmaus account is primarily a proof of the resurrection of Jesus. The report of the empty tomb by the women was not sufficient to convince the two disciples of the resurrection. Jesus was regarded as "a prophet mighty in work and word" (v. 19), one who was to be the deliverer of Israel except that his untimely death has cast a doubt in their minds of his messianic role. They were oblivious of the necessity of the Messiah to suffer before entering into glory, which led to their rejection of the report about his resurrection. On their way to Emmaus, they encountered the risen Lord who rebuked their skepticism, clarified their understanding of Scriptures, and finally removed the veil from their eyes, enabling them to recognize him. Garland says, "A prophet mighty in deed and word inadequately express who Jesus is. If John is more than a prophet (7:26), Jesus is much more. Now he is the resurrected Lord."[35]

Second, the Christocentric focus of Scripture is seen in this passage. The divine salvific plan of God is known through Scriptures. Luke portrays the prophetic role of Scripture in this account. What had happened to Jesus of Nazareth was a fulfillment of Scripture. The prophets in the Old Testament foretold his suffering, death, burial, and resurrection. Paul would later defend the resurrection of Christ by pointing to the Scriptures. He says, "For I handed down to you as of first importance what I also received, that Christ died for our sins according to the Scriptures, and that He was buried, and that He was raised on the third day according to the Scriptures" (1 Cor 15:3–4 NASB). Furthermore, the theological conviction that all Scripture is christological in focus is affirmed in Luke 24:44, "Now he said to them, 'these are my words which I spoke to you while I was still with you, that all the things that are written about Me in the Law of Moses and the Prophets and the Psalms must be fulfilled'" (NASB). In the words of Dillon, "He alone is the definitive revelation of the whole Bible's meaning."[36]

---

35. Garland, *Luke*, 958. Also, Bock holds that the account functions as a summary to provide assurance about resurrection. God can work through crucifixion because it is followed by resurrection. See Bock, *Luke 9:51–24:53*, 1923.

36. Dillon, *From Eye-Witnesses*, 205.

Third, the Emmaus account validates the identity of Jesus as a prophet and suffering Messiah. On the road to Emmaus, when Jesus asked the two disciples about the things that happened in Jerusalem, they replied, "Things concerning Jesus of Nazareth, who was a prophet mighty in work and word before God and all the people, and how our chief priests and leaders handed him over to be sentenced to death and had him crucified" (vv. 19–20). Alan C. Mitchell notes that "Luke's portrayal of Jesus as a prophetic Messiah and Mark's presentation of the suffering Messiah comes to a fuller expression in the Emmaus narrative, which nicely joins Jesus' identities as prophet and suffering Messiah."[37]

## Conclusion: Implications for Preaching

According to R. Bruce Bickel, Protestants for the most part have lost their confidence in one of the greatest assets of their tradition: the mysterious, creative power of the word of God proclaimed from the pulpit.[38] This diminishing view of the supernatural nature of preaching is because preachers do not see clearly the unique and supernatural nature of Holy Scripture.[39] In addition, Bickel asserted that many preachers do not have a clear conviction about the nature of preaching. They "share" rather than "preach," pray rather than pronounce blessings, and perform under a clouded vision of their ministry.[40] From the exegetical analysis, some implications for preaching will be delineated that will focus on the importance of the Scriptures in preaching and the prophetic nature of preaching.

First, a Spirit-empowered witness is Christocentric in focus. From the text, Jesus stressed to the two disciples walking to Emmaus and later to all the disciples that all the Scriptures speak of him. If Scripture is christological

---

37. Mitchell, "Prophet Mighty in Deed," 333–34. Also, Mitchell asserts that it is true that all the Synoptic Gospels portray Jesus as this long-awaited Messiah; each does that in its own distinctive way. Even if they share common broad elements and use similar titles such as Son of Man, Son of God, and the Christ (the Anointed One), the individual authors offer different portraits of Jesus that reflect how each defines him as the Messiah. Whereas Mark stresses the role that suffering plays in Jesus's messianic destiny, Matthew focuses on Jesus as a royal Messiah who will restore David's kingdom, and Luke joins a prophetic dimension to the notion of a royal Messiah as a way of explaining the necessity of Jesus's suffering and death. See Mitchell, 329.

38. Bickel, *Light and Heat*, 1.
39. Bickel, 1.
40. Bickel, 1.

in focus, preaching as witness should be the conviction of every preacher, which is to bear witness to Christ (the foundation of prophecy). The angel said to John, "For the testimony of Jesus is the spirit of prophecy" (Rev 19:10 NASB). John the apostle captured the witnessing role of John the Baptist by saying John came to testify about the light (John 1:7). John was the last of the prophets before Christ and first of the witnesses. He was the precursor of the Messiah, pointing his very finger and saying, "Behold, the Lamb of God" (John 1:36). Indeed, prophecy has been transformed by the coming of Jesus Christ but it is still in operation. Adrian Hastings writes:

> Witness is rooted in prophecy, and therefore the latter, though necessarily transformed by the coming of the Christ and the fullness of time, did not disappear but in a new form remained at the center of the life of God's Israel, the disciples of Jesus. Our Lord's possession of the Spirit, his prayer, and his gift of prophecy were all passed on in full measure to the Christian community.[41]

Today, preachers of the Christian community stand like the Old Testament prophets bearing witness to the works and teachings of Christ. In addition, the Spirit has come to join the voices of the Old Testament prophets and preachers today to bear witness to Christ (John 15:26–27).

Second, a Spirit-empowered witness is mighty in words and works. Spirit-empowered preaching is not in words alone – rather, it is with words and works. Paul says to the Thessalonians, "For our gospel did not come to you in word only, but also in power and in the Holy Spirit and with full conviction; just as you know what kind of men we proved to be among you for your sakes" (1 Thess 1:5 NASB). O'Reilly said, "Word and sign are complementary and only their combined witness authenticates the preaching of the missionary as the word of God."[42] Jesus of Nazareth, a prophet, mighty in words and works was the testimony of the two disciples walking to Emmaus. When Jesus sent

---

41. Hastings, *Prophet and Witness*, 97.

42. O'Reilly, *Word and Sign*, 194. In addition, O'Reilly goes on to affirm that signs and wonders are subordinate to the word. The signs and wonders are means, the preaching of the word the end. The apostles will be able to preach more boldly if their word is effective in healing and working miracles of exorcism when they invoke the name of Jesus. These signs will demonstrate the mighty power of their words and show that it transcends all human capabilities and categories, that is, in short, the word of God. O'Reilly, 194.

out the twelve and the seventy, he gave them power to preach and to heal the sick (Luke 9:2; 10:9). Thus, the disciples were empowered to be mighty in words and works, and they returned with news of fruitfulness (9:6; 10:17).

Therefore, preachers need to pray to God to authenticate their message with mighty works like healing, deliverance, conversion, etc. I am not advocating exhibitionism, works pointing only to themselves or the preacher; rather, works authenticating the gospel message. Luke stated in Acts how the believers apparently prayed for signs to confirm their message (4:30) and to grant them boldness to preach (4:29). God answered their prayer by filling them again with the Spirit (4:29–31). In addition to authenticating the gospel, mighty works also encourages the witness to continue preaching the word boldly, even in the face of persecution (4:29–31; 14:2–3).[43]

Third, a Spirit-empowered witness impacts the audience. The prophetic character of the word and work is what makes preaching supernatural. Isaiah 55:11 says, "So will My word be which goes out of My mouth; it will not return to Me empty, without accomplishing what I desire, and without succeeding in the purpose for which I sent it" (NASB). The prophetic word will always produce extraordinary results: it brings about repentance, forgiveness of sins, confidence, healing, deliverance, just to mention a few. In the Emmaus discourse, the prophetic word brought conviction to the hearts of the two disciples. They said, "Were not our hearts burning within us as he spoke to us on the road, as he opened the Scripture?" O'Reilly believes that Luke sees a parallelism between the word of the Old Testament prophets and the New Testament apostles and successors. The word preached by the prophets and apostles has a noetic aspect, which denotes an intelligible content, and a dynamic aspect indicating that the word could affect the change it signified.[44]

---

43. Luke pointed to many examples of how signs or mighty works authenticated the Gospel in Acts. In Samaria, the Samaritans heeded Philip's preaching specifically because of his miracles (8:6–7). A large population in Judea was converted because of signs (9:34–35, 40–42); so were the Roman governor (13:9–12) and the Philippian jailer (16:29–30). In Ephesus, many responded to the preaching of Paul because of his miracles and other mighty works (19:11–20), and in Malta, although Paul was a captive, his healing ministry led to public honor (28:8–10), which led to some responding in faith.

44. O'Reilly, *Word and Sign*, 215. Also, O' Reilly says the word/sign duality is carried from the Old Testament, through Jesus, to the apostles and missionaries on the vehicle of prophetic succession. It is one of the many devices used by Luke to highlight the continuity between the ministry of Jesus and that of the preachers of the infant church, and between the new era

This is what the Puritan preachers were concerned about. Bickel says, "The Puritan's concern was light and heat – light from the Word of God to penetrate the darkness of the heart and soul of the hearer, heat from the pathos and passion of the heart and soul of the preacher to bring about conviction."[45]

Thus, Spirit-empowered preaching operates in this dynamism. It was the Spirit that inspired the words of both the prophets and apostles. Witnessing without the power of the Spirit will be fruitless. Consequently, Jesus said to his disciples, "You are witnesses of these things. And behold, I am sending the promise of My Father upon you; but you are to stay in the city until you are clothed with power from on high" (Luke 24:48–49 NASB). If the Old Testament prophets, apostles, and early church depended on the empowerment of the Spirit to witness, it implies that the postmodern preacher is not an exception to this rule.

Finally, a Spirit-empowered witness believes in human responsibility. A prophet "mighty in words and works" implies a divine reality and human action as well. More will be said in chapter 6 about human responsibility; thus, there is no need to belabor the issue here. However, it is vital to comment about the aspect of the preacher's personal discipline in the word. One does not become mighty in words by trusting in the Spirit alone; there is need for the discipline of voracious study of the word. Paul says to Timothy, "Study to shew thyself approved unto God, a workman that needeth not to be ashamed, rightly dividing the word of truth" (2 Tim 2:15 KJV). A life of dependence on the Spirit should lead one to a conscientious reading and meditation of the Scriptures daily. Azurdia says, "The issue for the preacher is not study or the Spirit, as though a wedge can be driven between the two. It is study and the Spirit."[46]

Apart from the preacher's responsibility, the audience has a responsibility as well. They are to respond positively to the preaching of the word. After Cleopas and his colleague recognized Jesus during supper, they believed in the

---

of salvation represented by these and the period of the promise represented by the law and prophets of the Old Testament. O'Reilly, 216.

45. Bickel, *Light and Heat*, 30. Heisler says, "A preacher's head and heart must meet together in the Holy Spirit to produce powerful preaching that informs the mind, inflames the heart, moves the will, and transforms the life." See Heisler, *Spirit-Led Preaching*, 10.

46. Azurdia III, *Spirit Empowered Preaching*, 139.

resurrected Christ, and they responded positively by returning to Jerusalem to rehearse their transformation. The writer of Hebrews says, "For indeed the gospel was preached to us as well as to them; but the word which they heard did not profit them, not being mixed with faith in those who heard it" (Heb 4:2 NKJV).

CHAPTER 4

# Luke's Testimony about Jesus: Acts 1:1–5

The assumptions made in chapter 2 are applicable in this chapter as well. For the sake of clarity, some of the assumptions will be reiterated here.[1] First, the assumption that Luke-Acts are two volumes that are inseparable is assumed here, too. The Gospel of Luke and Acts are two parts of what was intended as a single literary composition. Second, the view that Luke the evangelist is the author of both books and that he wrote to a Christian audience (Theophilus and friends) is also assumed. Third, this work will not assume any source theory for the composition of Acts. Finally, since authorship is disputed, so too is the date of composition; two options have dominated the discussion of the date of composition. One option is sometime in the AD 60s, and the other is AD 70–100.[2] Rather than entering this debate, it is best to go with Marshall's conclusion. For Marshall, the lack of interest in the fall of Jerusalem in Acts and the way in which the book ends its story before the death of Paul are strong indications of a date before AD 70; however, a date not far off AD 70 appears to satisfy all requirements.[3]

---

1. Virtually all the assumptions are debatable.
2. Richard I. Pervo has a good list of scholarly estimates of the date of Acts composition. See Pervo, *Dating Acts*, 359–63. Although Pervo proposed that evidences from his research pointed to a date AD 115, or 110–120, he believed that the current consensus that would date Acts AD 85 represents more of a political compromise than a hypothesis established by rigorously examined and argued criteria. See Pervo, 343.
3. Marshall, *Gospel of Luke*, 35.

This chapter presents an exegetical analysis of Acts 1:1–5. The goal of this work is threefold: (1) to establish the testimony of Luke about the ministry of Jesus as it relates to words and works; (2) to ascertain some theological themes from the passage; and (3) to deduce some implications for preaching from the text. We are fully aware that Acts has a number of characteristics that are unique and fascinating. Prominent among these is the narrative form, which is the dominant literary form. As predominantly narrative, Liefied notes that the most detailed exegesis of a narrative still does not turn it into a doctrinal declaration; however, meaning can be drawn.[4] Our goal is not detailed exegetical work, but exegesis that is sufficient to support the thesis of this research. The rest of the unique characteristics and features of Acts will be discussed in the historical and literary section of this work.

## Historical Context

Novelists use titles that catch the attention of prospective readers. On the other hand, scholars desire titles that will give an accurate description of the purpose and contents of their books. According to Richard Pervo, the best-attested title for this book is "Acts of the Apostles" (πραξεις ἀποστόλων).[5] Pervo traced the historical meaning of "Acts" (πραξεις) to mean an account of the accomplishment of an important person, in this case, the apostles.[6] Thus, Luke was writing to a Christian audience (Theophilus and his friends) giving an account of the apostles' accomplishments.

After the title discussion, the next subject regards the reliability of the text of the book of Acts. Although the goal of this analysis is not text-critical, one must provide some basic comments about the text if one is to engage in exegetical work. Keener is on target when he notes that the book of Acts provides the thorniest text-critical situation in the New Testament.[7] From the earliest times, several or at least two, editions of the book were in circulation:

---

4. Liefeld, *Interpreting*, 15.

5. Pervo, *Acts*, 29. According to Fitzmyer, this title is found in the best Greek manuscripts (P⁷⁴, ℵ, ψ, B, D, 1, 1175). Sometimes the title appears at the end of the Greek text, as in P⁷⁴: *Praxis [ap]ostolon*. See Fitzmyer, *Acts of the Apostles*, 47. Also, the title "Acts of the Apostles" appears widely by the end of the second century. See Keener, *Acts: Introduction*, 645.

6. Pervo, *Acts*, 29.

7. Keener, *Acts: Introduction*, 7–8.

the Alexandrian and the Western forms. The Alexandrian was shorter and traditionally regarded as the authentic text of Acts. Metzger notes that the Western text is nearly one-tenth longer than the Alexandrian text.[8] Many theories have been proposed as to the relationship between the two forms of Acts, but that is not the focus of this study.[9] The point of this discussion is to say that the inquiry about the relationship between the Alexandrian text and the Western edition is in reality ambiguous, as Ernst Haenchen asserts.[10] Therefore, apart from the textual rendering in verse 5, the analysis in this study will use the eclectic form edited by the UBS[5] committee.[11]

Turning to a consideration of the purpose of Acts, Luke wrote to Theophilus and his friends to tell them of the story that embraces both the work of Jesus and of the followers of Jesus after his ascension.[12] On the one hand, Luke in his Gospel wanted to reassure Theophilus of the truth he had learned. He wrote, "So that you may know the exact truth about the things you have been taught" (Luke 1:4). Maddox noted that it is a work aimed at reassuring the Christian community about the significance of the tradition and

---

8. Metzger, *Textual Commentary*, 223.

9. For theories on the relationships between the two texts, Metzger has a significant summary of scholarly discussion. See Metzger, *Textual Commentary*, 223–32.

10. Haenchen, *Acts of the Apostles*, 56. He went on to explain why he thinks it is ambigous. He noted that the expression "Western text" does not have one clear and invariable meaning. It may denote (1) the text that we already encounter in Marcion, Tatian, and Irenaeus, and that is clearly everywhere, in East and West, the product, albeit by no means uniform, of elucidations and of explanatory or occasionally pious interpolations and expansions; There is not reason to call this a "recension" – this text is not and never was a unity. But "Western text" may also denote (2) the revision to which a thoughtful, painstaking, and erudite reader – already using a "Western text" in the first sense subjected our book, removing seams and gaps and inserting a detail here and there. Finally (3) it may denote those variants that sometimes resemble Aramaisms but are no more nor less than the careless mistakes of a scribe (or two successive scribes), working *ca.* 500, mistakes that have added a special flavour to one particular codex based on the "Western" text in the first two senses. Consequently, Haenchen concluded that in none of these three cases does the "Western text" of Acts provide us with the "original" text. That is the lesson we have been in gradual process of learning. See Haenchen, *Acts of the Apostles*.

11. On the grounds that there is no hypothesis thus far proposed to explain the relationship between the two forms of Acts, the United Bible Societies' Committee produced an eclectic edition. Metzger reviewed the work of the committee on the book of Acts and observed that more often than not the shorter, Alexandrian text was preferred. At the same time the committee recognized that some of the information incorporated in certain Western expansions may well be factually accurate, though not deriving from the original author of Acts. See Metzger, *Textual Commentary*, 235.

12. See chapter 2.

faith in which it stands.[13] On the other hand, Luke in the Acts of the Apostles narrated what the followers of Jesus did as witnesses. Marshall points out that Luke presented Acts in the form of the story of how the church received and obeyed the command to bear witness to Jesus.[14] A specific reason why Luke wrote Acts as complementary to the Gospel is not clearly stated in the opening verses of Acts. Therefore, any suggestion is speculative and should not be pressed too hard. A number of theories have been proposed.[15] All these theories are plausible, and they also prove the diversity and richness of the book of Acts.

Liefeld points out that one of the ways a reader receives help in seeking theological revelation in a biblical narrative is by identifying with the author.[16] Since Acts is predominantly narrative, I am of the opinion that by identifying with Luke in the prologue of both Luke and Acts, one is able to gain some light to authorial intent. More so, the name Theophilus appears in both prologues (Luke 1:3 and Acts 1:1). Also, since the majority of scholars agree that Luke-Acts is a single unit, then it makes sense to connect the purpose of the two books together via the prologues. Marshall connects the two books and asserts that Theophilus is first given an account of the life of Jesus as to confirm the truth of the gospel, and then an account of how the

---

13. Maddox, *Purpose of Luke-Acts*, 186. In addition, Maddox held that the story of Jesus, and apostles, and the growing church is a story of "fulfillment" in more than one sense. On the one hand, Luke encourages his readers not only to look forward with hope to the consummation of all things at the end, but also to appreciate that "salvation," the grace and power of God in action, is a present reality, in which they already stand because of God's action in sending Jesus to the earth. On the other hand, they are to be reassured that this fulfillment has taken place "among us," within the Christian community. Furthermore, with such a message of reassurance, Luke summons his fellow Christians to worship God with whole-hearted joy, to follow Jesus with unwavering loyalty, and to carry on with zeal, through the power of the Spirit, the charge to be his witnesses to the end of the earth. See Maddox, *Purpose of Luke-Acts*, 187. Also, Liefeld made similar comments. He pointed that Theophilus has some knowledge of the gospel of Christ. Luke 1:4 indicates that Luke is writing so that this person (and the group he represents) may have "assurance" concerning the things of which they had already heard. Liefeld, *Interpreting*, 25.

14. Marshall, *Acts of the Apostles*, 44.

15. Here are some proposals regarding purpose: (1) To provide the church with a record of its beginning; (2) a careful historical account; (3) an evangelistic purpose; (4) an apologetic value; (5) the identity of the people of God; and (6) to provide a paradigm for Christian evangelism, missions, and church life. See Liefeld, *Interpreting*, 30–32.

16. Liefeld, *Interpreting*, 59. Besides identifying with the author, Liefeld stated three other ways. First, setting the passage in its larger context. Second, the characters in the narrative, beyond serving as moral exemplars, will illustrate the "ways of God" as he works in the lives of those who do or do not believe and obey him. Third, the movement of the narrative and even the time construction become teaching tools. Liefeld, *Interpreting*.

disciples bore witness to him in a way which confirms its truth.[17] Therefore, we are affirming that witness to Jesus is the primary purpose of Acts, and all other proposals about purpose can fit under it.[18] Luke emphasized that this witnessing to Jesus is by words and deeds.[19]

## Literary Context

Most scholars today believe that the book of Acts is organized on the programmatic statement in 1:8, which listed the geographical locations where the apostles were to bear witness. Jesus said, "And you shall be my witnesses both in Jerusalem, and in all Judea, and Samaria, and as far as the remotest part of the earth" (Acts 1:8 NASB). In spite of this consensus, they still differ over the structure of the book.[20] On grammatical grounds, one is justified to take Judea and Samaria as one unit since only one article is used for the two locations. Thus, we affirm the threefold structural outline of Acts (Jerusalem,

---

17. Marshall, *Acts of the Apostles*, 44. Similarly, Talbert's comment is reminiscent of Marshall's statement. He writes,

> When one concentrates on the foreground of Luke-Acts, three matters come to mind. First, what is the plot of Luke and Acts? The plot of Luke is simply put: conceived, empowered, and guided by the Holy Spirit, Jesus both embodies the Way and makes provision for others to follow in it, thereby fulfilling the divine plan. The plot of Acts is equally straightforward: between the ascension and parousia, empowered by the Holy Spirit, the Messianists bear an unstoppable, universal witness to Jesus by word and deed, thereby fulfilling the divine plan. Here the focus is on the church but against the background of the divine plan.

See Talbert, *Reading Acts*, 4.

18. In fact, according to Steven Ger, the dozen plausible reasons that have been proposed over the centuries as to the purpose of Acts (i.e. historical purpose, theological purpose, apologetic purpose, and biographical purpose) all point to one theme, namely, witnessing to Jesus. See Ger, *Book of Acts*, 10. Stewart Custer also made similar assertion – see Custer, *Witness to Christ*, xviii–xxi.

19. C. F. D. Moule also summed up the concept of "witness" of Acts under the general heading of deeds or action. He asserts that there are three ways of witness described in Luke's story. They are: the witness of deeds or action, the witness of words, and the witness of community life. According to him, these three are also seen in the writing of Peter (1 Pet 2:9, 12; 3:15). Furthermore, they are also seen in later history with the friars, such as the Dominicans or Franciscans, with their deeds of mercy, their preaching, and their loyalty to their communities. See Moule, *Christ's Messengers*, 16–17.

20. Some scholars proposed a threefold structural outline of Acts. See Conzelmann, *Act of the Apostles*, 7; Martin, *All About Witnessing*, 10; Marshall, *Acts of the Apostles*, 29; Lenski, *Interpretation of the Acts*, 15. J. C. O'Neill proposed a fivefold structural outline; see O'Neill, *Theology of Acts*, 72. Gerhard Krodel proposed a twofold division; see Krodel, *Acts*, 6–8.

Judea/Samaria, and the ends of the earth). Following the threefold proposal of Marshall, the book of Acts can be divided as illustrated: witnesses in Jerusalem (1:1–5:42); witnesses in Judea and Samaria (6:1–11:18); and witnesses to the ends of the earth (11:19–28:31).[21]

Theological wealth deposited in the book of Acts is conspicuous as one ventures into interpretation. One way to study the book is either by an inductive or deductive study of major themes within the book. The first theme that becomes obvious in the book of Acts is the Holy Spirit. In the opening chapter alone, which is predominantly the post-resurrection instruction, the Holy Spirit appears four times (1:2, 5, 8, 16). Other references to the Spirit are ubiquitous in the book of Acts: in connection to the inspiration of Scripture (4:25; 28:25); the ministry of the apostles and disciples (4:8; 6:3, 5; 7:55; 11:24; 13:9; 20:22); the judgment on Ananias and Sapphira (5:3, 9); the leading of Philip (8:29, 39); the conversion of Paul (9:17); the acceptance of the Gentiles (10:45–47; 15:8); the commissioning of Paul and Barnabas for mission (13:2, 4); the decision of the Jerusalem council (15:28); the guidance of mission work (16:6, 7; 20:22); and in the various prophecies recorded (20:23; 21:4, 10–11). This led Liefeld to the conclusion that if the narrative of Acts teaches theology at all, it teaches that the Holy Spirit is regularly active among God's people in this age.[22]

Acts 1:1–5 is located in the Jerusalem section. Luke 24 ends with the disciples gathered in Jerusalem with the risen Christ. The story continues from there with the post-resurrection instructions. Talbert writes, "In Luke 24, the instruction and the ascension function to close the time of Jesus' earthly ministry; in Acts 1, they function to lay the foundation for the ministry of the church that is about to begin."[23] The last paragraphs of Luke 24 and the first few paragraphs of Acts 1 speak of Jesus not only instructing his disciples through the Holy Spirit (Acts 1:2), but also reappearing to them in many ways, giving them proof of his resurrection (1:3). Also, it was during that period

---

21. Marshall, *Acts of the Apostles*, 29. Marshall notes that the points of demarcation are debatable, but his structure attempts to plot the flow of the narrative. At the same time, there are loose ends in the story that do not appear to be entirely due to the storyteller's art, but leave the reader puzzled in the wrong sense. Marshall, *Acts of the Apostles*.

22. Liefeld, *Interpreting*, 84.

23. Talbert, *Reading Acts*, rev. ed., 1–2.

that the risen Christ reminded his disciples about the coming of the Spirit shortly after his departure (1:4–5).

## Exegesis of Acts 1:1–5

The exegetical work in this study will rely mostly on the UBS[5] edited edition of the text of Acts, which is based on the Alexandrian text. In verse 5, the eclectic edition of the UBS[5] rendered the prepositional phrase as, ἐν πνεύματι βαπτισθήσεσθε ἁγίῳ based on the Alexandrian witnesses. However, I will adopt βαπτισθήσεσθε ἐν πνεύματι ἁγίῳ (Western witnesses), for the sake of unity.[24] There are six textual variants in the passage to be considered; however, none of these affects the meaning of the text. The analysis that follows will divide the text into two sections: Luke's testimony of Jesus's ministry (vv. 1–2); and Luke's testimony of the post-resurrection ministry of Jesus (vv. 3–5).[25]

### Luke's Testimony of Jesus's Ministry

> In the first book, O Theophilus, I treated all that Jesus began to do and also to teach, until the day he was taken up, after he had instructed through the Holy Spirit the apostles whom he had chosen. (vv. 1–2)

Luke begins the account of the witness of the disciples to Christ with a reference to his previous work. The phrase "In the first book" (Τὸν μὲν πρῶτον λόγον), refers to the Gospel of Luke. C. K. Barrett was quick to point that the use of Τὸν πρῶτον does not necessarily imply that Luke intended to write more than two volumes.[26] Thus, it is logical that a sequel should begin with a brief synopsis of the first part. He stated the name of the recipient of his

---

24. The Alexandrian rendering has more emphasis than the Western text by fronting βαπτισθήσεσθε. However, the reason why we adopt the Western reading is because the Jordan event in Luke 3:16 has the same phraseology in Acts 1:5 as rendered by Western text. The Western text harmonized the sequence of words in Acts 1:5 to parallel the report in the Synoptic Gospels, all of which place ἐν πνεύματι ἁγίῳ after the word βαπτισθήσεσθε (Matt 3:11; Mark 1:8; and Luke 3:16). See Metzger, *Textual Commentary*, 243. In addition, Metzger believed that the UBS[5] Committee preferred the Alexandrian text because it is superior to the Western text. See Metzger, *Textual Commentary*.

25. We are following John B. Polhill's structure. See Polhill, *Acts*, 77. Note, the text is one verse in the Greek and it is difficult to structure.

26. Barrett, *Critical and Exegetical*, 65.

first book, namely Theophilus. This implies that he is writing or dedicating this book to the same person as in the Gospel of Luke (1:3). Also, it is the first parallel connection between the two books, which further signifies a continuation of the same story and with the same goal in view. But unlike the Gospel of Luke, where the title "most excellent" (κράτιστε) was attached to Theophilus, here the title was omitted. R. C. H. Lenski suggested that the title was omitted in Acts because Theophilus had now become a Christian as a result of the gospel account, and thus it was seen improper for a Christian to address a fellow Christian with such a title.[27]

After the preface, Luke goes on to state briefly a summary of the Gospel of Luke. First, he begins with the utmost brevity in the last clause of verse 1 "All that Jesus began to do and also to teach." The two complementary infinitives (ποιεῖν/διδάσκειν) are joined together by a coordinating conjunction, "and also" (τε καὶ), to give a vivid description of the ministry of Jesus. Fitzymer noted that this phrase is a description of Jesus's deed of healing and words of instruction during his ministry, a summary of the impact that Jesus made, such as Luke has narrated in his Gospel (5:15; 6:18; 9:11; cf. 24:19).[28] Consequently, one is justified in asserting that Luke's goal in the Gospel was to show the works and words of Jesus. He was able to state this through the two disciples walking to Emmaus who confessed that Jesus was a prophet mighty in word and work (Luke 24:19). Barrett noted that ποιεῖν and διδάσκειν seem a very adequate summary both of the contents and of the interests of the third Gospel; he also argued that Matthew had a special interest in διδάσκειν, while Mark focused more on ποιεῖν.[29]

Second, Luke pointed out the absolute dependence of Jesus on the Holy Spirit even after his resurrection. In verse 2, there is a construction known as an internally headed relative clause, where the head noun "day" (ἡμέρας) is actually inside the relative clause (ἄχρι ἧς ἡμέρας) that modifies it, though the

---

27. Lenski, *Interpretation of the Acts*, 21.

28. Fitzmyer, *Acts of the Apostles*, 195.

29. Barrett, *Critical and Exegetical*, 66. Similarly, Lenski believed that the gracious and mighty miracles of Jesus (ποιεῖν) and the gracious and true teaching of Jesus (διδάσκειν) had won Theophilus, who was either a Roman knight or Roman official or a man of very great prominence, to faith. Luke's Gospel had scored a great missionary success. See Lenski, *Interpretation of the Acts*, 21. Also, according to Bruce, as the Gospel records what Jesus began to do and teach (cf. Luke 3:23), so Acts records what he continued to do and teach, by his Spirit in the apostles, after he was "taken up." See Bruce, *Acts of the Apostles*, 98.

noun gets its case from the main clause (i.e. the preposition ἄχρι).³⁰ Instead of the "typical" Koine construction, which would have been (ἄχρι ἡμέρας ἧς) as in 1:22, Luke did otherwise here. According to Culy and Parsons, the construction was for the purpose of intensifying the expression: "until the very day."³¹ Luke was indicating that until the very day Jesus was taken up to heaven, he (Jesus) "through the Holy Spirit" (διὰ πνεύματος ἁγίου) was instructing his disciples, thus implying that Jesus was depending on the Holy Spirit prior to his death and even after his resurrection.³²

## Luke's Testimony of the Post-Resurrection Ministry of Jesus

> To them also he had presented himself living after he had suffered, by many convincing proofs, appearing to them over forty days and speaking things about the kingdom of God. And being assembled, he commanded them not to leave Jerusalem, but to await the promise of the Father, which "You heard from me, for John, on the one hand baptized with water, but in a few days you will be baptized with the Holy Spirit." (vv. 3–5)

Luke is the only writer in the New Testament that specifically mentions the forty days duration of the post-resurrection appearances of Jesus. He goes on to write of Jesus's final instruction to the disciples after his resurrection. Before the final instruction, Jesus gave his disciples convincing proofs of his resurrection. In verse 3, the construction "After he had suffered" (μετὰ τὸ παθεῖν αὐτὸν), a preposition with an infinitive is used to indicate antecedent time, that is, the event of the infinitive precedes the event of the main verb, which in this case is "presented" (παρέστησεν).³³ The suffering of Jesus

---

30. Culy, Parsons, and Stigall, *Acts*, 3.
31. Culy, Parsons, and Stigall, 3.
32. I took the prepositional construction with the genitive "Through the Holy Spirit" (διὰ πνεύματος ἁγίου) as modifying ἐντειλάμενος rather than ἐξελέξατο because of word order. Culy and Parsons stated that for it to modify ἐξελέξατο it would have to follow the relative clause οὓς, which marks a clause boundary. See Culy, Parsons, and Stigall, *Acts*, 3. A similar view was held by scholars such as Fitzmyer, *Acts of the Apostles*, 196; Barrett, *Critical and Exegetical*, 69; Keener, *Acts: Introduction*, 661. Polhill, *Acts*, 81. On the other hand, there are those who propose that the genitive should be taken with the "choosing" (ἐξελέξατο) of the apostles. See Larkin, *Acts*, 38; Haenchen, *Acts of the Apostles*, 139. The problem with this view, however, is that it forces the Greek text, and there is no mention of the Spirit in the choice of the apostles in Luke 6:12–13. See Fitzmyer, *Acts of the Apostles*, 196.
33. Wallace, *Greek Grammar*, 594.

preceded his resurrection. Also, his death was included in the suffering, which is an example of a synecdoche.³⁴ Jesus presented himself alive with many irrefutable "proofs" (τεκμηρίοις) to his disciples over forty days.³⁵ Luke in the Gospel had already given some examples of these proofs: the empty tomb (24:1–12), the Emmaus road (24:13–32), the appearance to Peter (24:34), and the appearance to the entire group (24:36–43). Polhill writes, "The appearances to the apostles are absolutely essential for their primary role in Acts of being witnesses to his resurrection (1:22; 2:32; 3:15; 5:32; 10:39–41; 13:31)."³⁶

After giving the disciples sufficient proof of his resurrection, he also reminded them about the thrust of his ministry. He taught his disciples about the kingdom of God, which was the central focus of his earthly ministry. Jesus said in Luke 4:43, "I must preach the kingdom of God to the other cities also, for I was sent for this purpose." Luke did not explain in the above verse what the kingdom of God meant. He assumed that the reader would know what it meant. The same applies here in Acts as well. C. H. Dodd in his legendary work *The Apostolic Preaching and Its Developments* says, "The kingdom of God is conceived as coming in the events of the life, death, and resurrection of Jesus, and to proclaim these facts, in their proper setting, is to preach the Gospel of the kingdom of God."³⁷ Interestingly, just like the phrase "kingdom of God" appears here in the beginning of Acts, the same phrase would appear at the conclusion of Acts (Acts 28:23, 31). Bruce says, "So in Acts 8:12; 28:23, 31 (cf. 20:25) the kingdom of God is closely associated with 'the story of Jesus'

---

34. Culy, Parsons, and Stigall, *Acts*, 4.

35. BDAG, s.v. "τεκμηρίον." Also, Aristotle defined τεκμηρίον as conclusive sign. By conclusive signs he meant statements that are irrefutable. See Aristotle, *Rhetoric*, 13.

36. Polhill, *Acts*, 81.

37. Dodd, *Apostolic Preaching*, 24; Bock, similar to Dodd, asserts that God's kingdom refers to God's promised rule that comes with Jesus's messianic program and activity. See Bock, *Acts*, 55. Notwithstanding, there are some who hold a wider view of the kingdom of God. According to Barrett, the phrase "kingdom of God" has a wider use in Luke and Acts. It is a future good, for whose coming men may pray (Luke 11:2), as they did in Judaism (Luke 23:51). It is near at hand (Luke 10:9, 11). In the presence of Jesus and his work it may be said to have come already (Luke 11:20). It is God's gift to his own, who manifest that they are his own (Luke 6:20; 9:62; 12:32), and though they suffer now they will enjoy the gift when the appointed time comes (Luke 13:28, 29; cf. Acts 14:22). It is impossible to answer the question when the kingdom will come (Luke 17:20). It is an inward, spiritually possessed thing (Luke 17:21). See Barrett, *Critical and Exegetical*, 71.

(τὰ περὶ τοῦ Ἰησοῦ)."[38] Thus, preaching and teaching about the kingdom of God framed the entire book of Acts.

Luke then focused on the final instruction of Jesus to his disciples in verse 5. Jesus charged his disciples to remain in Jerusalem for the promise of the Father in verse 4. This is reminiscent to what he said in Luke 24:49, "And behold, I am sending the promise of my Father upon you; but you are to stay in the city until you are clothed with power from on high" (NASB). Thus, Luke links the end of his Gospel to the beginning of Acts. For Luke, then, "the promise of the Father" is going to be the source of empowerment for mission. This he emphasizes both in the conclusion of his Gospel and here in the introduction to Acts, which shows how pivotal it is for Luke's theology of the divine mission.[39] Luke uses a *hoti* (ὅτι) clause in verse 5 to reiterate for the sake of more explanation why the disciples must wait in Jerusalem for the promise of the Father. He cites Jesus referring his disciples back to John's prophecy about his mission in order to ground his charge to them: "John responded to them all, saying, 'As for me, I baptize you with water; but He is coming who is mightier than I, and I am not fit to untie the straps of His sandals; He will baptize you with the Holy Spirit and fire'" (Luke 3:16 NASB). By evoking John's prophecy, Jesus was grounding his charge (to wait for the promise of the Father). Furthermore, he was affirming his messianic credential because according to John, the gift of the Spirit was the sign that the Messiah had come (Luke 3:15–16). Keener holds that "Luke omits here [in v. 5] the parallel description of Jesus bringing 'fire' because judgment is not immediately relevant in this context."[40]

What then is "the promise of the Father?" Luke in verse 5b used the future verb, "You will be baptized" (βαπτισθήσεσθε) to affirm the soon coming promise of the Father. For one to be "baptized" means to cause someone to have an extraordinary experience akin to an initiatory water-rite.[41] In this case, the Holy Spirit is the instrument of this baptism. Luke identifies "The promise of the Father" mentioned in verse 4 as the Holy Spirit in this verse (v. 5). He goes on in verse 8 to explain the purpose of the Spirit's coming,

---

38. Bruce, *Acts of the Apostles*, 100.
39. Keener, *Acts: Introduction*, 675–76.
40. Keener, 678.
41. BDAG, s. v. "βαπτίζω."

which is primarily to empower the disciples for witness. He writes "But you will receive power when the Holy Spirit has come upon you; and you shall be my witnesses both in Jerusalem, and in all Judea and Samaria, and even to the remotest part of the earth" (v. 8). And Luke would later affirm Jesus to be the baptizer with the Spirit (2:33).

The phrase "baptism of the Spirit" has generated much debate among evangelical Christians.[42] Baptism of the Spirit is one of the many imageries Luke used to speak about the profound experience of the Holy Spirit in believers.[43] I interpret the baptism of the Spirit here to mean one of the distinctive blessings of the new age, which will result in Spirit-empowered prophetic witness in mighty words and works.[44] The position assumed in this

---

42. Michael Green summarized the three main positions in contemporary scholarship about the baptism of the Spirit. First, there are those who identify baptism in the Holy Spirit with water baptism. The second view holds that baptism with the Spirit is identical with conversion (mostly Protestant and evangelical churches). The third view has a two-stage initiation. It comes with a divided voice from two different backgrounds: the Catholic view (stage one, baptism, is incomplete; stage two, confirmation, brings the Holy Spirit into a person's life), and the Pentecostal view (conversion as stage one, and subsequent overpowering experience of the Holy Spirit accompanied by speaking in tongues as stage two). Green affirmed the second view held by many evangelical churches. See Green, *I Believe in the Holy Spirit*, 159–63. A good resource that advocates the evangelical view is by James Dunn. He argues that for the writers of the New Testament, the baptism in or gift of the Spirit was part of the event (or process) of becoming a Christian, together with the effective proclamation of the gospel, belief in Jesus as Lord, and water-baptism in the name of the Lord Jesus. See Dunn, *Baptism in the Holy Spirit*. On the other hand, a good resource from the Pentecostal view that critically reviewed Dunn's work is by William P. Atkinson, *Baptism in the Spirit: Luke–Acts and the Dunn Debate*.

43. Talbert noted that Luke used various images to describe the experience of the Holy Spirit. When the experience is viewed from the angle of divine initiative, it is spoken of in terms of the Spirit's being given (5:32; 8:20; 10:45; 11:17; 15:8), being poured out (2:17–18; 2:33; 10:45), coming on people (1:8; 19:6), and falling on people (8:16; 10:44; 11:15). When viewed from the point of view of the people experiencing the Spirit, it is spoken of in terms of receiving the Spirit (2:38; 8:15, 17, 19; 10:47; 19:2), being filled with the Spirit (4:31; 9:17; cf. 6:5; 11:24), and being baptized with the Spirit (1:5; 11:16). These various modes of expression are referring to the same experiential reality: for example, in the story of Cornelius five of the terms are clearly used interchangeably: give the Spirit (10:45; 11:17), pour out the Spirit (10:45), Spirit fell on (10:44; 11:15), receive the Spirit (10:47), and be baptized with the Spirit (11:16); in Acts, 2:4 (filled with the Spirit) fulfills 1:5 (be baptized with the Spirit). It is this experiential reality, spoken of in variety of ways that will enable the disciples' ministry. Until they are so empowered, as Jesus had been (Luke 3:21–22; 4:18–21), they are to wait in Jerusalem. See Talbert, *Reading Acts*, rev. ed., 8.

44. I am not advocating a two-stage initiation experience for believers today like the Pentecostal church would argue. For believers today, the baptism of the Spirit happens at conversion not a subsequent experience after conversion. However, the apostles' experience was in two distinct stages. John Stott pointed out that the 120 were regenerate already, and received the baptism of the Spirit only after waiting upon God for ten days. He went on to clarify that the fact that the experience of the 120 was in two distinct stages was due simply to historical

work is grounded on three reasons. First, in chapter 2, we have argued that Jesus's baptism was an empowerment with the Spirit to inaugurate the era of salvation through his mighty words (preaching) and deeds. In addition, Jesus in this verse parallels his baptism in the Jordan River with what the disciples are about to experience. Second, Jesus explicitly described the result of the baptism of the Spirit in verse 8 and Luke 24:49 as empowerment for witnessing. Finally, Peter interpreted the Pentecostal experience as a fulfillment of Joel's prophecy that foreshadowed the inauguration of the last days, where the Spirit would be poured out to all flesh for the purpose of prophesying.

Similarly, O'Reilly saw a parallel connection between the baptism of Jesus as foreshadowing that of the disciples and concluded that:

> As a baptism, the Pentecost event is the inauguration of the ministry of Jesus' disciples. As a baptism with the Spirit – the same Spirit which had descended upon Jesus in the Jordan – it is a prophetic anointing for a ministry of preaching and healing, a ministry characterized by powerful word and mighty deed. Even a casual glance at the Acts of the Apostles will confirm that this indeed is how the ministry of the Apostles and missionaries is presented.[45]

Although similar, there is a slight difference. For O'Reilly, and others like Menzies, the baptism with the Spirit is a prophetic anointing for missions only. However, we see a prophetic anointing for missions as an offshoot of the baptism of the Spirit. Thus, the prophetic anointing is one of the many blessings that came with the Spirit at Pentecost. Hence, the disciples would be baptized with the Spirit in a few days. It is by means of the Spirit's power that the disciples would be able to preach the kingdom of God, and thus fulfill their mission of witnessing to Christ. In sum, John's baptism was preparatory for the Spirit baptism. J. H. E. Hull said it well, "Water-baptism had prepared

---

circumstances. We today live after the event of Pentecost, like the 3,000. With us, therefore, as with them, the forgiveness of sins and the "gift" or "baptism" of the Spirit are received together. See Stott, *Baptism & Fullness*, 28–29.

45. O'Reilly, *Word and Sign*, 43. O'Reilly believed that the Spirit for Luke is intimately linked with speaking or preaching the word. See O'Reilly, 51. Other advocates of this view are Menzies, *Empowered for Witness*, and Shelton, *Mighty in Word*.

a community for the New Age; Spirit-baptism would produce the community of the New Age."[46]

## Theology of the Passage

Acts 1:1–5 is an introduction to the book of Acts. It reviews the forty-day post-resurrection period of Jesus. During this period, the risen Lord appeared on numerous occasions to his disciples, giving them final instructions (vv. 1–2). Also, the text highlights some key themes of the book, especially the theme of the Holy Spirit (vv. 3–5). Commenting on verses 3–5, Gordon J. Keddie says, "Luke sums up this teaching under two general headings: the kingdom of God and the baptism of the Holy Spirit."[47] Thus, from the exegetical analysis, three theological themes can be observed from the text.

First, there is a clear theme of the resurrection of Jesus. Luke says in verse 3, "To them also he had presented himself living after he had suffered by many convincing proofs." The proof of resurrection was crucial for the apostolic witnesses (Luke 24:44–48). In fact, it was one of the criteria used to fill up the apostolic position of Judas (Acts 1:21–22). Although no Christian today is required to be an eyewitness to the resurrection, it is nevertheless imperative for one to affirm a belief in the resurrection to become a Christian. Paul writes, "But if there is no resurrection of the dead, then not even Christ has been raised; and if Christ has not been raised, then our preaching is vain, your faith also is vain" (1 Cor 15:13–14 NASB).

Second, embedded in verse 3 is the theme of the kingdom of God. Luke says that after the resurrection, Jesus went about speaking things about the kingdom of God. The risen Lord was not teaching any new doctrine besides the one he taught during his ministry. The Lukan phrase "kingdom of God" is akin to Matthew's "kingdom of heaven." Simply put, the kingdom of God is the rule of God in the works and person of Christ. Mark J. Beach insightfully defines the kingdom of God; he writes, "The kingdom of God is his

---

46. Hull, *Holy Spirit*, 45. Similarly, Polhill said, "Unlike John's baptism, the new converts would also receive the presence and power of the Holy Spirit (2:38b). Throughout Acts new converts experienced repentance, baptism, and the gift of the Spirit. All three are essential elements of the conversion experience." See Polhill, *Acts*, 83.

47. Keddie, *You Are My Witnesses*, 12.

redemptive, restorative, healing, returning-to-fellowship reign – and all this in, through, and because of the person and work of Jesus Christ."[48]

Third, the theme of the baptism of the Spirit is explicitly stated in the text (vv. 4–5). Barrett said, "The Holy Spirit is one of the major themes of Acts; some would say the central and most important theme."[49] John had already spoken about the baptism of the Spirit and that Jesus will be the baptizer (Luke 3:16). In fact, one can trace the idea of the baptism of the Spirit in the Old Testament (Ezek 36:25–27; Isa 44:3). Luke would later affirm Jesus as the baptizer with the Spirit in the sermon of Peter. He quotes Peter saying: "Therefore, since He has been exalted at the right hand of God, and has received the promise of the Holy Spirit from the Father, He has poured out this which you both see and hear" (Acts 2:33 NASB). Fitzmyer writes, "Such a baptism will thus be the Spirit principle by which Jesus' followers will live their new lives and bear witness to the risen Lord. The Spirit will be the dynamo that activates their testimony."[50]

Undoubtedly then, the baptism of the Spirit is mainly for the purpose of witnessing to Jesus. In view of other New Testament teaching, it should be noted here that the baptism of the Spirit as the apostles experienced it is not the norm for today. John Stott notes that the 120 disciples' experience of the Holy Spirit was in two distinct stages due to historical circumstances, which will not be repeated.[51] Thus, like the three thousand converts that responded to the preaching of Peter, believers today receive the baptism of the Spirit at conversion. This is why Paul says, "For by one Spirit we were all baptized into one body, whether Jews or Greeks, whether slaves or free, and we were all made to drink of one Spirit" (1 Cor 12:13 NASB). This is not to say that there are no other experiences of the Spirit on an individual subsequent to conversion because Acts 4 clearly shows subsequent fillings of the Spirit on

---

48. Beach, "Kingdom of God," 54. Also, Michael J. Vlach saw Jesus as the focal point of the kingdom of God from a Pauline point of view. He pointed out that the term "kingdom" is used sparingly by Paul, but there are important truths concerning the kingdom in his letters. For Paul, Jesus is the center of God's kingdom plan and one must believe in him to inherit the kingdom. As for its nature, the kingdom of Jesus the Messiah is future and earthly from Paul's standpoint in history, yet there are kingdom truths that apply to Christians in this age before Jesus returns and the kingdom is established. See Vlach, "Kingdom of God," 59.

49. Barrett, *Critical and Exegetical*, 74.
50. Fitzmyer, *Acts of the Apostles*, 204.
51. Stott, *Baptism & Fullness*, 29.

the disciples. I am affirming the broad teaching of the Scriptures that there is one baptism but there can be many infillings of the Spirit. Robert M. Tenery and J. Steve Sells sum it well: "While there is one baptism of the Spirit, there are many infillings of the Spirit . . . the disciples who had received the Holy Spirit in the upper room (John 20:20) received an even greater infilling on the day of Pentecost."[52]

In sum, Hull asserts that there are four things that Luke wanted to convey about the Spirit in the first chapter of Acts: (a) that his recipients may receive a new power in their lives which will enable them to become like Christ; (b) that those who receive the Spirit may effectively communicate the gospel: in other words, this new power the Spirit brings is not merely for the personal benefit of its possessor nor is it simply moral power; (c) that through the Spirit a new community may be born of those who are united with Christ and with each other; and (d) as a sign that the new age has dawned and a sign to those who possess the Spirit that they are partakers of this age.[53]

## Conclusion: Implications for Preaching

First, Spirit-empowered preaching demands a response from the audience. The kingdom of God theme assumes an invitation. After the temptation in the wilderness, Jesus returned to Galilee in the power of the Spirit, and he went on preaching and teaching in the synagogues (Luke 4:14–15). The content of his sermon was not stated, however in Mark's parallel account, the content was highlighted. Mark says, "Now after John had been taken into custody, Jesus came into Galilee, preaching the gospel of God, and saying, 'The time is fulfilled, and the kingdom of God is at hand; repent and believe in the gospel'" (Mark 1:14–15 NASB). From the content of Jesus's preaching, it is

---

52. Tenery and Sells, *With Greater Power*, 64. Also, Stott noted that the result of this baptism of the Spirit was that "they were all filled with the Holy Spirit" (Acts 2:4). Thus, the fullness of the Spirit was the consequence of the baptism of the Spirit. The baptism is what Jesus did (pouring out the Spirit from heaven); the fullness is what they received. The baptism was a unique initiatory experience; the fullness was intended to be the continuing, the permanent result, the norm. As an initiatory event the baptism is not repeatable and cannot be lost, but the filling can be repeated, and in any case needs to be maintained. If it is not maintained, it is lost. If it is lost, it can be recovered. The Holy Spirit is "grieved" by sin (Eph 4:30) and ceases to fill the sinner. Repentance is then the only road to recovery. See Stott, *Baptism & Fullness*, 48.

53. Hull, *Holy Spirit*, 47.

clear that Spirit-empowered preaching demands a response from the audience. This is not because the preacher gives an invitation; rather, it is because of the nature of the word. The writer of Hebrews says, "For the word of God is living and active and sharper than any two-edged sword, and piercing as far as the division of soul and spirit, of both joints and marrow, and able to judge the thoughts and intentions of the heart" (Heb 4:12 NASB). The preached word under the empowerment of the Spirit forces people to make a decision. Luke illustrated this in Peter's Pentecostal sermon when he says those who heard were "pierced to the heart, and said to Peter and the rest of the apostles, 'Brethren, what shall we do?'" (Acts 2:37 NASB). O'Reilly notes that the word preached by Peter was powerful and effective that penetrated into the depths of the hearers and forces them into a decision to accept or reject it.[54] Thus, Spirit-empowered preaching calls for immediate decision – it offers an invitation for people to respond.

Second, Spirit empowerment today is conditional on obedience. Luke clearly expressed that Jesus gave his disciples a command to wait on the Spirit (Luke 24:49; Acts 1:4). Part of their preparation for ministry was that they learn the discipline of lingering on the Spirit. Jesus tarried for thirty years before starting his ministry. Little was said about this period of waiting; however, it is clear from Scriptures that throughout Jesus's life, he was waiting on his Father's timing (Mark 1:15; John 2:4; 7:6). Also, it was during the waiting period that Luke stated that Jesus increased in wisdom and in stature (Luke 2:52). In the same way he had waited on the Father's timing, Jesus instructed his disciples to wait for the baptism of the Spirit. If the disciples had gone fishing instead of heeding his command to wait in Jerusalem for the Spirit, chances are they would have missed the baptism of the Spirit on the day of Pentecost. Luke was emphatic about obedience as a condition for receiving the Spirit. He says, "And we are witnesses of these things; and so is the Holy Spirit, whom God has given to those who obey Him" (Acts 5:32). Thus, according to Acts, the disciples waited patiently in prayer and fellowship (1:12–14). In addition, Luke in Acts implicitly narrated some instances where the disciples practiced the discipline of waiting on the Spirit (Acts 2:1; 13:2).

Therefore, there is a need for preachers to be obedient to the leading of the Spirit. One discipline that helps one to hear the voice of the Spirit is the

---

54. O'Reilly, *Word and Sign*, 73.

discipline of waiting on the Spirit. Forbes used the childbirth metaphor to describe the process of sermon development under the anointing of the Spirit. The Spirit is with the preacher in conception, gestation, and delivery of the sermon. Forbes includes another stage of preparation, writing, "Then we have to have the capacity to wait a while. Sometimes, the sermon won't come when we want it to come. We have to learn to wait on the Lord."[55] There is a need for the contemporary church and preachers to rediscover the discipline of waiting on the Lord. Isaiah 40:31 says, "Yet those who wait for the LORD will gain new strength; they will mount up with wings like eagles, they will run and not get tired, they will walk and not become weary" (NASB).

Third, Spirit-empowered preaching demands that the witness be filled with the power of the Spirit. After commanding his disciples to wait in Jerusalem for the Holy Spirit in verse 5, Jesus went on to tell them the implication of the Spirit upon their lives. It is the power of the Spirit upon their lives that would grant them effective witnessing. This is not a truth unbeknownst to the disciples because they have already experienced it. Luke recorded two occasions where Jesus gave his disciples power and sent them to preach and heal (Luke 9:1–6; 10:1–20). Right in the middle of these two events Luke inserted an incident where the disciples could not cast out demons from a boy until Jesus came to their rescue (9:37–45). On one occasion they could cast out demons (9:6; cf. Mark 6:7–13), but another time they were not able to do it. When they later asked him why it was that they could not cast the demons from the little boy, Jesus told them that it was possible only through prayer and fasting (Mark 9:28–29). This confirms that the work of the Spirit can be quenched in the life of a believer (1 Thess 5:19). It also implies that spiritual disciplines (prayer, fasting, meditating, etc.) are means of reviving depleted grace and power in a believer.

Another example that illustrates the need for continuing infilling of the Spirit is seen in Acts. In Acts 1:5, Jesus promised the coming of the Spirit on the disciples, and then in chapter 2, Luke records the fulfillment of that promise. However, in chapter 4, Luke noted that the disciples were praying for more of the Spirit's empowerment. Their prayers were answered, and they were filled again with the Spirit to preach boldly (4:25–31). Atkinson points out that the disciples' previous experience did not discourage them

---

55. Forbes, *Holy Spirit & Preaching*, 86.

from praying for renewed acts of power; in effect, they asked for more.⁵⁶ Therefore, there is need for believers, and especially preachers, to be filled with the Spirit daily. The imperative to be filled with the Spirit is not intended to be a one-time experience; it is expected to be an ongoing experience for believers, as the verb "be filled" (πληροῦσθε) is in the present continuous tense (Eph 5:18). In addition, the command to be filled demands an ethical response from all believers. It is not an option. Rather, it is an obligation to all believers. Tenery and Sells write, "A church can do little unless there is the power of the Spirit present. Spirit-filled people build great churches. People who care little about the presence of the Holy Spirit often maintain small, stagnant or dying churches."⁵⁷

Finally, a Spirit-empowered witness depends entirely on the Holy Spirit in every aspect of sermon preparation. Luke stated that until the day Jesus ascended to heaven, Jesus through the Sprit was instructing his disciples about the kingdom of God (v. 2). His earthly ministry started with his dependence on the Spirit and ended on the same note. This is why Zechariah said to Zerubbabel, "'Not by might nor by power, but by My Spirit,' says the LORD of armies" (Zech 4:6 NASB). Thus, Azurdia does not mince words when he says, "The power of the Holy Spirit is the *sine qua non* of gospel preaching, the one thing without which nothing else matters."⁵⁸

---

56. Atkinson, *Baptism in the Spirit*, 131–32.
57. Tenery and Sells, *With Greater Power*, 71.
58. Azurdia III, *Spirit Empowered Preaching*, 98.

CHAPTER 5

# Peter's Testimony about Jesus: Acts 10:34–43

This research set out to investigate Spirit-empowered preaching as demonstrated in the ministry of Jesus from the testimonies of three witnesses in Luke-Acts and from the testimony of Jesus himself. In the Old Testament framework, the testimony of three witnesses is sufficient to ratify any issue. Paul reminded the Corinthians that every fact is to be confirmed by the testimony of two or three witnesses (2 Cor 13:1). Apart from Jesus's testimony of his ministry, the testimonies of the two disciples walking to Emmaus, and that of Luke have already been investigated in the previous chapters. What remains now is to add the third testimony, which is the voice of Peter the apostle, who was the leader of the twelve apostles and one of three in the inner circle (with John and James) of Jesus. This chapter presents an exegetical analysis of the sermon of Peter in Acts 10:34–43. The goal of this investigation is threefold: (1) to establish the testimony of Peter about the ministry of Jesus as it relates to his anointing with the Holy Spirit; (2) to ascertain some theological themes from the passage that are relevant to Spirit-empowered witnessing; and (3) to delineate some implications for preaching.

## Historical Context

Historical context deals with the world behind the text:[1] authorship, date of composition, purpose of writing, recipients of the letter, and the author's

---

1. Kuruvilla, *Privilege the Text!*, 42. The concept of "the world behind the text," "the world of the text," and "the world in front of the text" is actually from Paul Ricoeur. See Kuruvilla, 39–42.

source(s). All these aspects have been discussed in the previous chapter; hence we will not revisit them. One characteristic of Acts that was discussed in the previous chapter is the narrative form. Although narratives are not explicitly turned into doctrinal declaration, nevertheless, doctrinal meaning can be implicitly drawn from them. Unlike the narratives, which are difficult to interpret, the speeches are less difficult. Furthermore, the speeches contain propositional statements, and so are more similar to the Epistles than the narratives.[2] Like the Epistles, the speeches call for careful attention to their context and to the shared assumptions between the speaker and the hearer.[3] A large percentage of the book of Acts is made up of speeches. Mark Allan Powell says, "Out of about 1000 total verses in the book of Acts, over 300 constitute speeches delivered by various characters."[4] These speeches are of different kinds. F. F. Bruce groups them into four groups: evangelistic, deliberative, apologetic, and hortatory.[5] The passage for exegesis falls under the evangelistic group, but before focusing on it, it is vital to comment briefly about the authenticity of these speeches.

Powell notes that in the first half of the twentieth century these speeches were considered as the most important part of the book of Acts because they represent the actual content of the gospel proclaimed by the apostles; however, most scholars today think the opposite: the speeches in Acts represent the portions of the book where Luke exercised his literary license most freely.[6] Martin Dibelius of Heidelberg spearheaded the latter movement. According to Dibelius,

> These speeches, without doubt, are as they stand inventions of the author. For they are too short to have been actually given in this form; they are too similar to one another to have come from different persons; and in their content they occasionally reproduce a later standpoint (e.g. what Peter and James say about the Law in chap. xv).[7]

---

2. Liefeld, *Interpreting*, 61.
3. Liefeld, 61.
4. Powell, *What Are They Saying*, 30.
5. Bruce, *Speeches in the Acts*, 5.
6. Powell, *What Are They Saying*, 30–31.
7. Dibelius, *Fresh Approach*, 262.

It is partly in response to this negative criticism of the speeches in Acts that F. F. Bruce wrote to adduce evidence to prove the validity of the speeches in Acts.

According to Bruce, Luke inherited the tradition of Greek historical writing handed down from the time of Herodotus and Thucydides in the fifth century BC.[8] One feature of that tradition was the composition of appropriate speeches for appropriate occasions by writers. Thucydides stated that he was not able to record all the speeches word for word in his memory, so he wrote, "My habit has been to make the speakers say what was in my opinion demanded of them by the various occasions, of course adhering as closely as possible to the general sense of what they really said."[9] However, later historical writers in the first century AD imitated the freedom of Thucydides without his historical conscience. Bruce notes that these historical writers were composing speeches freely and putting them into the mouths of their characters, not with any historical probability, but to show off their highest skill in literary composition.[10] That seems to be the fashion of the time that Luke was writing, and against this background he (Bruce) investigated the speeches in Acts.

Bruce was intrigued by the differences he observed. Furthermore, he compared the speeches in the third Gospel with their parallels in the other two Synoptists, who did not inherit the traditions of Greek historical writing. He concludes by saying, "On the basis of such a comparison, the general conclusion of Synoptic students is that Luke has preserved his Sayings source or sources with great faithfulness."[11] In view of what has been argued, I hold

---

8. Bruce, *Speeches in the Acts*, 6.
9. Thucydides and Crawley, *History of the Peloponnesian War*, 25.
10. Bruce, *Speeches in the Acts*, 7.
11. Bruce, 8. One thing that caught Bruce's attention was the form of writing. He says, "For an author who could write such idiomatic Greek as the prologue to the Third Gospel, the Greek of some of the speeches in Acts is surprisingly awkward." See Bruce, 8. Similarly, Conrad Gempf has a more detailed approach to this whole issue in the setting of the relevant ancient literature. He too came to the same conclusion as Bruce and suggested that we must stop approaching the speeches in Acts with a twentieth-century preconception and learn instead to view them in the setting of first-century literary conventions. This does not mean, as Dibelius thought, setting aside any connection between recorded speeches and historical referents. That is to misunderstand the first-century authors. One should think of the speeches in terms of the two-pronged concept of literary and historical appropriateness: the historians were interested in including speeches that were appropriate to their book and also appropriate to the alleged speaker and situation. Therefore, one must learn to think of the public speeches not as (accurate or falsified) transcript/summaries of the words of famous people, but rather as records (faithful or unfaithful) of historical events. See Gempf, "Public Speaking," 302–3.

that all the speeches in the book of Acts are faithful and trustworthy. Also, out of the several ways one can view a speech, we will study Peter's speech in terms of its content and themes.[12]

Within the four groupings of speech earlier stated, Peter's speech in Acts 10:34–43 falls under the evangelistic group. Bruce further subdivided the evangelistic group according to the nature of the audience. The method of presenting the good news to pagans was naturally different from how it was presented to those acquainted with the Old Testament, whether they were Jews or "God-fearers" – that is, Gentiles who had abandoned pagan worship and become "adherents" of the synagogue without becoming Jewish proselytes.[13] Thus, the latter kind of evangelistic oratory fits Peter's speech in the house of Cornelius.

Concerning the text and content of Peter's speech, C. H. Dodd writes, "The Greek of Acts 10: 35–38 is notoriously rough and ungrammatical, and indeed scarcely translatable, though the general meaning is clear. This is strange in so excellent a Greek writer as the author of Acts."[14] This is a strong evidence to support the fact that Luke translated an Aramaic document of Peter's speech instead of composing it himself. Bruce noted that whether Peter actually spoke in Aramaic on this occasion is immaterial; the point is that so far as the linguistic evidence goes, the accounts seem originally to have been preserved in an Aramaic document.[15] In spite of the poor grammar, Dodd proposed that the content of the speech offered explicitly a form of primitive apostolic preaching, namely, kerygma.[16] Although the theology of the speech is primitive, Bruce held that it is nonetheless essentially theological.[17]

---

12. Liefeld holds that a speech can be viewed in five ways: length; content and themes; context; style and composition; and function and significance. See Liefeld, *Interpreting*, 65–73.

13. Bruce, *Speeches in the Acts*, 5.

14. Dodd, *Apostolic Preaching*, 27. In fact, in Acts 10:36–38, Metzger noted that in several respects, the Greek of the Alexandrian text is harsh: (1) both sentences lack connecting particles; (2) ἀρξάμενος cannot be syntactically construed; and (3) the abrupt apposition of Ἰησοῦν τὸν ἀπὸ Ναζαρέθ to ῥῆμα is far from idiomatic. Besides several scribal efforts at amelioration, modern attempts to account for the unusual Greek include (1) the theory that an Aramaic original was translated literalistically into poor Greek (see the following comments); and (2) the suggestion that the text, being unrevised, is a conflation of two different drafts of essentially the same sentence. See Metzger, *Textual Commentary*, 333.

15. Bruce, *Speeches in the Acts*, 8.

16. Dodd, *Apostolic Preaching*, 28.

17. Bruce, *Speeches in the Acts*, 10.

## Literary Context

Acts 10:1–11:18 is believed to be the longest single narrative in all of Acts. This is due to the importance Luke placed on the mission to the Gentiles. Barrett noted the importance of this account:

> The importance of the story for Luke and for Luke's book is thus unmistakable. It marks the final critical stage in the extension of the Gospel and the expansion of the church. At first the Gospel is preached to and accepted by Jews; next it moves as far as Samaritans; then comes the devout Ethiopian, who is all but a proselyte, going on pilgrimage to Jerusalem and reading the Bible privately. Finally, there is Cornelius, on whose conversion even Jerusalem Christians, who at first object to Peter's dealings with an uncircumcised man, are obliged to remark, why then, to the Gentiles also God has granted repentance unto life (11:18).[18]

In like manner, Bock sees this section as a key element in Luke's legitimization of the church as a thriving institution that was designed for Jews and Gentiles by God's plan and direction.[19] The narrative can be divided into two broad sections: the encounter of Peter and Cornelius (10:1–48), and the report in Jerusalem about the gentile mission (11:1–18). The two sections are closely interwoven. Polhill notes that there is considerable duplication between the scenes; Cornelius's vision is told four times (10:3–6, 22, 30–32; 11:13–14), and Peter's vision is given in detail twice (10:9–16; 11:4–10).[20] He goes on to assert that all of 11:3–17 is basically a summary of chapter 10.[21]

Structurally, the first section, which is the encounter of Peter and Cornelius (10:1–48), is nicely organized. It begins with Cornelius having a vision to send emissaries to invite Peter who was in Joppa (10:1–8). Similarly, Peter receives a vision from the Lord instructing him to respond to the invitation (10:9–16). What follows is the meeting between Cornelius's emissaries with

---

18. Barrett, *Critical and Exegetical*, 491.
19. Bock, *Acts*, 380.
20. Polhill, *Acts*, 250. Furthermore, Polhill asserted that the repetition in these sections serves a twofold function. First, it makes for a vivid narrative; it is related in dialogue, which gives the reader a sense of "being there." Second, and more significantly, it underlines the importance of the event. It will be repeated yet a final time in Peter's testimony at the Jerusalem Conference (15:7–11). Polhill, *Acts*.
21. Polhill, *Acts*.

Peter, who accepts the invitation (10:17–23). Next, Peter goes with Cornelius's men to meet with their master, and when they met, they shared their visions with each other (10:24–33). This is followed by Peter's testimony about Jesus (10:34–43). Finally, the scene climaxes with the divine bestowal of the Spirit upon the Gentiles (10:44–48).

## Exegesis of Acts 10:34–43

Within the subsection of the Cornelius episode (chapter 10), Peter's testimony about Jesus (10:34–43), which is the focus of this work, is arguably the most important in the narrative because of its kerygmatic nature. Dodd writes, "The principal elements of the *kerygma* can be traced in this speech – the fulfillment of prophecy, the death and resurrection of Christ, His second advent, and the offer of forgiveness."[22] For the sake of exegesis, the passage will be divided into four units: the introduction to Peter's testimony (10:34–35); Peter's testimony of Jesus's early ministry (10:36–38); the apostolic testimony of Jesus's later ministry (10:39–42); and the prophetic testimony of the ministry of Jesus (10:43). The four verses in the Greek text support this outline. In addition, since the analysis is focusing on content and theological themes, Pervo suggests a content-based approach is preferable in this passage than a rhetorical structure, which is unlikely to fit the passage.[23]

### The Introduction to Peter's Testimony

> Then Peter opened his mouth and said, "Now I realize how true it is that God does not show favoritism, but in every nation the one who fears him and does what is right is acceptable to him." (Acts 10:34–35)

Luke begins the testimony of Peter with an important phrase, "then Peter opened his mouth" (Ἀνοίξας δὲ Πέτρος τὸ στόμα). He is fond of using this kind of phrase to introduce a weighty statement. It was used in 8:35 where Philip preached Christ to the Ethiopian eunuch, and it occurs again in 18:14, where

---

22. Dodd, *Apostolic Preaching*, 27.

23. Pervo, *Acts*, 277. Pervo's theme in the passage is universalism. And he proposed a symmetrical structure: the universal God (vv. 34b–36); the mission of Jesus (vv. 37–40); the apostolic mission (vv. 421–42); and the universal judge (vv. 42b–43). Pervo, *Acts*, 277.

Paul was about to address Gallio, the deputy of Achaia. Also, the phrase is a solemn expression with biblical roots (Job 3:1; Matt 5:2).[24] Peter's new discovery is a theological truth in relation to the situation he just observed. The verb "realize" (καταλαμβάνομαι) is a verb of knowing, which means to come to understand something that was not understood or perceived previously.[25] Consequently, this understanding was circumstantial from what had just transpired (10:1–33). Marion L. Soards noted that speeches are often initially focused on the situation, but here the real concern is the statement about the universal character of God.[26] Peter's theological insight is that God does not show favoritism. The word "favoritism" (προσωπολήμπτης) appears only here in the New Testament and it means God is not one who shows partiality; he does not single out the Jews, but he also allows the Gentiles to come and receive salvation.[27] Barrett noted that the word "favoritism" is constructed on a Hebrew idiom meaning "to raise up the face," hence to show favor.[28] The main idea is that God does not make distinctions in his dealings with people.

Luke further emphasized that God does not show favoritism in verse 35. The prepositional phrase "in every nation" (ἐν παντὶ ἔθνει) was fronted for emphasis. For Peter, God's favor could be done even if one is not a Jew. This is similar to the words of Paul in Romans 3:29, "Or is God the God of Jews only? Is He not the God of Gentiles also? Yes, of Gentiles also." Luke used two substantive participles to describe the one that is acceptable (δεκτὸς) before God. The first is "the one who fears" (ὁ φοβούμενος) him. Already in verse 2 Luke described Cornelius as one who fears God and thus implies that God is not biased in this case because Cornelius is qualified. The second is "the one who does what is right" (ἐργαζόμενος δικαιοσύνην). Again, Luke presented

---

24. Bock, *Acts*, 395; Fitzmyer, *Acts of the Apostles*, 462; Barrett, *Critical and Exegetical*, 519.

25. Culy, Parsons, and Stigall, *Acts*, 209. Bullinger translated verse 34 thus, "I perceive (i.e., I now understand and am made to know from what has taken place) that God is no respecter of persons." See Bullinger, *Figures of Speech*, 553.

26. Soards, *Speeches in Acts*, 72.

27. TDNT, s.v. "προσωπολήμπτης." Also, BDAG, s.v. "προσωπολήμπτης."

28. Barrett, *Critical and Exegetical*, 519. The verb is used only in this verse in the New Testament; nevertheless, its cognates are used in the writings of Paul and James (Rom 2:11; Eph 6:9; Col 3:25; Jas 2:1). Barrett noted that although Peter shares the word cognate with Paul in this verse, their emphasis is different. Paul took up the expression from the primitive church. Peter recognizes that a Gentile may be as good as an Israelite, and be treated by God with equal favor; Paul is compelled against his natural wish to recognize that Jews, like Gentiles, are sinners in God's eyes. Barrett, 519.

Cornelius in verses 2, 4, and 22 as a man of godly character towards God and people. However, by no means should one interpret a salvific action from this. If that were the case, then what was the point of sending Peter to preach to Cornelius? Salvation is received through belief in Jesus. We agree with Bock that the point is not that Cornelius earned righteousness as his due (Rom 4:5) but that his responsiveness leads God to send Peter to reveal more of God's way to him, as the rest of the speech points the way to what Cornelius now must do.[29]

## Peter's Testimony of Jesus's Early Ministry

> As to the word that he sent to the children of Israel, proclaiming peace through Jesus Christ, who is Lord of all. You know what happened throughout all of Judea, beginning from Galilee after the baptism that John preached. How God anointed Jesus of Nazareth with the Holy Spirit and power, who went around doing good and healing all who were oppressed by the devil, because God was with him. (10:36–38)

The testimony of Peter begins with a review of the ministry of Jesus. Many commentators have noted the complexity of the syntax in this section.[30] Nonetheless, the meaning of the text is not affected. Luke begins reviewing Peter's speech with an accusative noun at the head of the sentence. According to Bullinger, when the accusative stands alone at the beginning of a sentence like in verse 36, it is to be rendered "as for" or "as to."[31] This kind of construction is known as the anacoluthon (non-sequence), and it is used for the sake

---

29. Bock, *Acts*, 396. Also, Bruce says,

> While divine salvation is according to grace (cf. 15:11), the undeviating principle in divine judgment is "to every one according to his works" (cf. Rom 2:6; Rev 20:1f), and is so stated throughout the Bible, from Gen 4:7 ("If you do well, will you not be accepted?"). Peter's [speech] is of great importance in introducing the role of God-fearing Gentiles in Luke's account of the expansion of Christianity.

See Bruce, *Acts of the Apostles*, 261.

30. Barrett asserted that the language of verses 36–37, and to some extent also verse 38, is so difficult as to be untranslatable. However, the general sense indeed is reasonably clear. See Barrett, *Critical and Exegetical*, 521; Also, for more discussion, see Fitzmyer, *Acts of the Apostles*, 463; Culy, Parsons, and Stigall, *Acts*, 210. Bruce, *Acts of the Apostles*, 262.

31. Bullinger, *Figures of Speech*, 721.

of emphasis or elegance to catch and fix the attention of the reader.[32] Peter presents his speech after arresting the attention of Cornelius and his audience. He speaks of "the word" (τὸν λόγον) that was sent to the children of Israel. Peter is referring to the gospel, which is the apostolic message. Luke then clarifies the content of the word as a message of "peace" (εἰρήνην), which echoes Isaiah 52:7 and 57:19. Keener pointed out that preaching "peace" in Isaiah meant good news that God was no longer angry with his people; Luke's use, which is informed by so-called Deutero-Isaiah as a whole, presumably means good news of reconciliation to and peace with God.[33] Peter is clearly affirming the universal offer of God's peace to humanity. In his article "Εἰρήνην, an Underlying Theme in Acts 10:34–43," Robert F. O'Toole argues that peace underlies the whole speech of Peter and so means God's universal openness to those who fear him and do what is right.[34]

Next, Peter declares the herald of this peace in the last clause of verse 36. God sent the message of peace through Jesus Christ. In a parenthetical and emphatic statement, Peter summarized the identity of Jesus. He described Jesus, the herald of peace, as "Lord of all" (πάντων κύριος). Soards held that the proclamation of Jesus as Lord occurs explicitly in 2:36 and 10:36 and implicitly in 22:8 and 26:15, which is but one form of statement about the theological identity of Jesus.[35] Indeed, this title speaks of the christological theme in Peter's speech, which implies that Jesus has been exalted by God and is Lord over all people, including Gentiles like Cornelius and his family. Polhill says, "Where Christ is Lord of all, a worldwide witness and a

---

32. Bullinger, *Figures of Speech*, 721.

33. Keener, *Acts, 3:1–14:28*, 1799.

34. O'Toole, "Εἰρήνην, an Underlying Theme," 475. In sum, O'Toole holds that in Acts 10:34–43, "peace" carries most of the meanings and nuances attributed to it elsewhere by Luke. In addition to God's universality (Luke 2:14, 29–32; cf. 12:51; Acts 7:26; 15:33; 16:36), forgiveness of sins (Luke 1:76–79; 7:47–50), the message about Jesus (10:5–6; cf. 24:36), his doing good (19:42; cf. Acts 9:31) and miraculous activity (Luke 8:47–48; 19:38; cf. 11:21), peace in this speech is God's salvific action (Acts 10:34–36; cf. Luke 1:68–79; 2:14, 29–32), and messianic, since it is achieved through Jesus (the) Christ, who is thus "Lord of all." Finally, "peace" for Luke is, not only a result of salvation, the spiritual and psychological state that follows on the reception or effect of God's salvific activity but rather another expression for salvation like forgiveness of sins. For Luke, Christian "peace" does not exist without the nuance of salvation. However, the particular nuance of "peace" finds itself in the various effects that other expressions of salvation achieve in and for the human being, be this between the individual and God, among individuals as in the case of universality or in the given individuals themselves. See O'Toole, 475–76.

35. Soards, *Speeches in Acts*, 73.

worldwide fellowship of believers free of all cultural prejudice are absolutely imperative."[36] Since, God does not show partiality (favoritism), those sent to witness to Christ are called to shun prejudices of every kind.

In verses 37–38, Peter now looks at the early ministry of Jesus as a whole, as indicated by the constative aorist participle, "what happened" (τὸ γενόμενον ῥῆμα) throughout all Judea.[37] He is going to trace the major steps of God's operation through Jesus. Also, he is going to appeal to the audience's general knowledge about the public ministry of Jesus that started from Judea after his baptism by John the Baptist. He assumes their awareness; hence he says, "you know" (ὑμεῖς οἴδατε) what happened throughout all of Judea. According to Keddie, Jesus's teaching and his healing ministry were well-attested and were common knowledge among the Gentiles in Palestine.[38] The first thing Peter noted about the public ministry of Jesus was the anointing of Jesus by God. He says in the first clause of verse 38, "How God anointed Jesus of Nazareth with the Holy Spirit and power." The "anointing" (ἔχρισεν) refers back to the Jordan incident (Luke 3:22) where the Spirit descended on Jesus like a dove. In his Nazareth sermon, Jesus interpreted his baptism as his anointing (Luke 4:18). Fitzmyer noted that although the gospel tradition never speaks of the baptism of Jesus by John as an "anointing," Luke so interprets it here.[39] Jesus's anointing presumably means that God made him Christ (Acts 4:27). Furthermore, the phrase with "the Holy Spirit and power" (πνεύματι ἁγίῳ καὶ δυνάμει) makes emphatic the feature of the anointing that was so obvious in his ministry. The Spirit and power has come upon his human nature. The connection of the Spirit and power are seen also in Acts 1:8; 6:5, 8, and 10. Barrett sees in this phrase a kind of hendiadys (the power of the Spirit); God bestowed the Spirit upon Jesus and as a result he was filled with power.[40]

---

36. Polhill, *Acts*, 261.

37. Barrett, *Critical and Exegetical*, 522.

38. Keddie, *You Are My Witnesses*, 130.

39. Fitzmyer, *Acts of the Apostles*, 465. Similarly, O'Reilly observed Acts 10:38 as interpreting the baptism of Jesus as God's anointing him with the Holy Spirit and with power. The same understanding of Jesus's baptism as an anointing is found in the words of Isaiah 61, which Luke places on the lips of Jesus in the synagogue of Nazareth. In addition, O'Reilly held that the baptism of Jesus is messianic anointing, but he saw prophetic anointing as well. See O'Reilly, *Word and Sign*, 30.

40. Barrett, *Critical and Exegetical*, 524.

Hence, Jesus was not only made Christ, but also, he was filled with power for his messianic ministry.

The second thing Peter noted about the early ministry of Jesus was the works of Jesus. Luke in the second clause of verse 38 uses two participles of manner to describe some of the consequences that followed Jesus's anointing. He says, Jesus went around "doing good" (εὐεργετῶν), and he went about healing (ἰώμενος) all who were oppressed by the devil. Luke recorded many good deeds of Jesus in his Gospel account. He also took careful accounts of healings and deliverances from demonic oppression that Jesus performed (Luke 4:33–36, 41; 8:26–39; 9:37–42; 11:14). Luke was the only evangelist to narrate the healing of the woman that was kept bound by a spirit of infirmity for eighteen years. She was healed in the synagogue on a Sabbath day, which infuriated the ruler of the synagogue. Jesus rebuked the ruler and said, "And this woman, a daughter of Abraham as she is, whom Satan has bound for eighteen long years, should she not have been released from this bond on the Sabbath day?" (Luke 13:16). In sum, Bock writes, "Jesus' good work of healing and ministry was that of one who served and benefited humanity."[41] In this speech, it can be implied that Luke is identifying Jesus as a prophet mighty in works.

Finally, in the last clause of verse 38, Peter indicated the source of Jesus's powerful ministry. Luke used a causal clause to state the reason Jesus's ministry was so powerful in words and works. He said it is "because" (ὅτι) God was with him. It was the powerful presence of God in Jesus that enabled him to be a mighty prophet. Luke used this same phrase (God was with him) in the speech of Stephen, where he (Stephen) ascribed the rise of Joseph in Egypt to the fact that God was with him (Acts 7:9). Besides Jesus and Joseph, Luke applied this expression to others in the book of Acts as well (11:21; 14:27; 15:4; and 18:10). Barrett stated that the phrase claims that Jesus was a man whom God accompanied and aided, as he was said to have accompanied and aided Abraham, Moses, or David.[42]

---

41. Bock, *Acts*, 398.
42. Barrett, *Critical and Exegetical*, 525.

## The Apostolic Testimony of Jesus's Later Ministry

> And we are witnesses of everything he did in the country of the Jews and in Jerusalem. Whom they also killed him by hanging him on a tree, this man God raised him on the third day and caused him to be visible, not to all the people, but to us, witnesses, who were chosen by God beforehand, who ate and drank with him after he rose him from the dead. And he commanded us to preach to the people and to testify that he is the one appointed by God to be judge of the living and the dead. (Acts 10:39–42)

Peter continues his testimony of the ministry of Christ by focusing on the later phase. He appeals to apostolic witnesses to validate his claim in verse 39. Peter used a generic first-person plural "we" (ἡμεῖς), referring to himself and the other disciples, especially the remaining ten and later Paul, as those who were commissioned by the Lord to serve as witnesses to these facts (Luke 24:48; Acts 1:8, 22; 2:32; 3:15; 5:32; 10:41; 13:31; 22:15; 26:16). The theme of witness is a central feature in Peter's preaching, which he would later emphasize in verse 41. For Peter, the apostles are eyewitnesses of all that Jesus did in the Jewish territory before and after his death.

Peter gives the apostolic testimony about the death and resurrection of Jesus Christ in verses 39b–40. He reiterates what he said earlier in his Pentecost speech (2:36). In brief, he attests to the fact that the Jewish authorities killed Jesus. However, God raised him up from the dead on the third day. Jesus was raised and made visible to witnesses. Barrett stated that it was God who granted to Jesus that he should thus be revealed, in addition to actually raising him from death.[43] Furthermore, the appearance of Jesus was not to all the Jewish people but to some chosen witnesses. In Acts, the apostles preached that Jesus's life and death was public knowledge to all in Jerusalem, but of his resurrection, "we are witnesses" (3:15; 5:32). These witnesses were "chosen beforehand" (προκεχειροτονημένοις) by God as in Acts 1:2; that he ate and drank with them recalls Luke 24:42–43, which together validate the concreteness of their testimony. Keener writes, "By reminding his audience

---

43. Barrett, 527.

of these matters, Luke stresses not only the reliability of Peter's claims in the narrative but also his own in his first volume."⁴⁴

Peter ends his testimony of the later ministry of Jesus by referring to Jesus's command for them to preach the gospel (Luke 24: 47–49; Acts 1:8). They were to preach (κηρύξαι) to all the people. The climax of their preaching is that Jesus is the one marked out by God as judge of the living and the dead. Lenski asserted that the deictic οὗτός in verse 41 is resumptive and gathers up all that Peter has said about Jesus: "he whom God anointed, etc., whom God raised from the dead and gave to be manifest as risen, who has been ordained and stands as thus ordained by God as judge of the living and dead."⁴⁵ This implies that Christ will judge people on the last day as to whether they accepted the apostolic testimony or not. The apostles, then, were eyewitnesses of Jesus's teaching, death, burial, and resurrection. In addition, they were also given the task of proclaiming Jesus as the soon coming judge of the living and the dead.

## The Prophetic Testimony of the Ministry of Jesus

> All the prophets bear witness about him that everyone who believes in him receives forgiveness of sins through his name. (10:43)

Peter concludes his testimony of the ministry of Jesus Christ by appealing to the witness of the prophets in the Old Testament in verse 43. In the first clause, Peter says, "All the prophets bear witness about him." Luke does not cite Peter quoting any prophetic passage. Most commentators assert that it is another instance of the Lukan global way of interpreting the Old Testament (Luke 24:25–27; Acts 8:35).⁴⁶ Although no prophetic text was cited, this statement

---

44. Keener, *Acts, 3:1–14:28*, 1806. Similarly, Pervo asserted that Luke integrates his proof with assertions about the divine plan; that is, this is an implied enthymeme, arguing from the events to God's intention. The language of "eating and drinking" conforms to Luke's unabashedly materialistic view of the resurrection, but its major function here may be to stress the intimacy and extent of the apostles' relationship with the risen Jesus. See Pervo, *Acts*, 281. In addition, Soards saw another function of the assertion that God chose those to whom the raised Jesus appeared and made them witnesses to the resurrection makes clear that the will and the direction of God control the dissemination of the news of the resurrection. The implication of this statement is that God operates with a "plan." See Soards, *Speeches in Acts*, 75.

45. Lenski, *Interpretation of the Acts*, 428.

46. Fitzmyer, *Acts of the Apostles*, 466; Keener, *Acts, 3:1–14:28*, 1808; Soards, *Speeches in Acts*, 76.

is a confirmation for the theme of witness to Christ in the Old Testament. Peter goes on to state the prophetic testimony that everyone who believes in Christ receives the forgiveness of sins through the name of Christ. Here Peter implied that faith in Christ is the condition required for salvation. Barrett writes, "The only qualification required is faith; it is not necessary to be, or to become, a Jew. Without saying so (and according to Luke's narrative without knowing that he has done so) Peter has prepared for what follows."[47] What followed was the pouring of the Holy Spirit upon Cornelius and members of his household, thus granting them the miracle of repentance and forgiveness (vv. 44–48). This incident occurred before Peter finished his speech. Soards noted that such interruptions indicate that the speaker has come to a convenient stopping point (see 2:36).[48]

## Theology of the Passage

This writer is arguing that Jesus's ministry models Spirit-empowered witness, which is demonstrated by mighty words and mighty works. Lischer writes, "Preaching is the final expression of theology."[49] He goes on to posit that after the exegete has told us what the text once meant, and the systematician has told us what the text means in its historical, doctrinal, and philosophical setting, the preacher then executes the text by helping it to speak to a particular time, situation, and people.[50] Consequently, some theological themes from the passage will be discussed before deducing some implications for preaching. Osvaldo Padilla holds that if this passage were to be disentangled, one could speak of three theological themes: (1) theodicy, (2) Christology, and (3) pneumatology.[51] Holding to these three themes, I will add the theme of witness to the list because it is an explicit theme in the text as well. Therefore, four theological themes are noticeable in this passage.

First, there is the theme of the universal offer of salvation. Luke in his Gospel makes clear that Jesus's ministry was not restricted to the Jews alone;

---

47. Barrett, *Critical and Exegetical*, 528.
48. Soards, *Speeches in Acts*, 76.
49. Lischer, *Theology of Preaching*, 14.
50. Lischer.
51. Padilla, *Acts of the Apostles*, 169.

he reached out to the Gentiles, the Samaritans, and other outcasts. On the contrary, Peter came to realize that God does not show favoritism at the house of Cornelius, a Gentile. He is not the God of Israel only; he is the God of the entire world. Liefeld says, "Thus Acts emphasizes the unity of God's people and the availability of the gospel to all. Within this ideal is the fact that Gentiles would eventually be more responsive (28:23–28)."[52] Salvation is not offered only to selected individuals; it is a gift to everyone. This is what the sending of the Holy Spirit meant: "But you will receive power when the Holy Spirit has come upon you; and you shall be my witnesses both in Jerusalem, and in all Judea and Samaria, and even to the remotest part of the earth" (Acts 1:8). Denton Lotz writes, "If God has no favorites, then God is not a tribal deity but the universal Lord who in Jesus Christ not only welcomes all but actively seeks them. That is why Peter after his dream gets up and goes to Cornelius. He acts upon his new perception of faith."[53] Luke sees salvation as a work of divine initiation that requires human response. God was the one that initiated the encounter between Cornelius and Peter, and while Peter was preaching, Cornelius believed and thus received salvation (Acts 11:1; 11:17). Marshall said, "Luke's task was to show what men everywhere must do in order to be saved."[54]

Second, there is the theological theme of witness. Luke presented Jesus as a Spirit-empowered witness in his Gospel. In this text, Peter affirmed that Jesus "went about doing good" throughout his ministry. One can see why John the apostle called Jesus the faithful witness (Rev 1:5). The theme of witness is also prominent in the book of Acts. Luke in this passage stressed the

---

52. Liefeld, *Interpreting*, 96.

53. Lotz, "Peter's Wider Understanding," 202.

54. Marshall, *Luke*, 215. Marshall traced this aspect of the synergistic approach to salvation in his work. He observed that the individual can do nothing to save himself. The initiative lies entirely in the hands of God. Throughout the writings of Luke it is God who takes the initiative in the work of his church; when the gospel is preached, it is at the behest of God (Acts 5:20), and the sending out of missionaries takes place by his command and guidance (Acts 8:26; 9:10–12; 10:19; 13:1–4; 16:6–10; 19:21; 20:22). The cumulative evidence of these passages is decisive. For Luke salvation is dependent upon the initiative of God who not only sends out the word but also prepares the hearts of men and women to receive it. Conversely, Marshall wrote about the human side of receiving salvation, where he affirms that the preaching of the word leads to the demand for response. He asserted that those who hear the word may accept it or reject it, the latter fulfilling with regard to themselves the prophecy of Isaiah 6:9. Through their rejection of the they word they cut themselves off from salvation. The response of those who accept the word is described as belief. See Marshall, 188–92.

evangelistic witness of the apostles and the Old Testament prophets. Peter saw his role as a witness to the events of the life and works of Jesus Christ. Lotz commenting on this passage writes:

> The apostles are called witnesses, as in Acts 1:8 and 22, 2:32, 3:15, 5:32, 13:31. To what do the apostles witness? To the earthly ministry of Jesus (v. 39) and to the cross and resurrection (vv. 39–41). The cross and resurrection are the content of the early church's preaching. This is the central content of God's revelation that attests and affirms the life of Jesus. Without the cross and resurrection, Jesus would have been a great religious teacher or preacher, but he would not have been Lord of all (cf. v. 36).[55]

In Acts there is a strong emphasis on the apostolic witness; however, witnessing is not confined to the twelve apostles. Every believer today is called to bear testimony to Christ because the Spirit of Christ inhabits every believer. Although believers today are not eyewitnesses of the events of the gospel, all believers are nonetheless called to bear witness to Christ on account of the prophetic and apostolic witness.

Third, the christological focus of the gospel (kerygma) is explicitly seen in this speech. Peter in this passage testified that Jesus was sent to the children of Israel proclaiming the gospel of peace. Jesus was a gospel-centered preacher who went about preaching the kingdom of God. In Acts, Luke presented Peter as a gospel-centered preacher also, who is christological in focus. All the speeches attributed to Peter in Acts are substantially similar. Dodd analyzed the first four speeches of Peter in Acts and observed that they supplement one another, and taken together they afford a comprehensive view of the content of the early kerygma. He summarized the primitive kerygma as follows: (1) the age of fulfillment has dawned; (2) this has taken place through the ministry, death, and resurrection of Jesus, of which a brief account is given with proof from the Scriptures; (3) by virtue of the resurrection, Jesus has been

---

55. Lotz, "Peter's Wider Understanding," 205. Also, Andrew C. Clark held that the role of the apostles as witnesses to the fact of Jesus's resurrection is clearly central for Luke. This role is stressed in their commissioning (Luke 24:48; Acts 1:8), and is seen to be central to their function in the account of the choice of Matthias to replace Judas (1:21). Peter continually refers to himself and his fellow apostles as witnesses to Jesus's resurrection in his speeches (2:32; 3:15; 5:32; 10:41; cf., also 4:2, 10, 33). They are also witnesses to Jesus's deeds in the country of the Jews and in Jerusalem. See Clark, "Role of the Apostles," 177–78.

exalted at the right hand of God; (4) the Holy Spirit in the church is the sign of Christ's present power and glory; (5) the messianic age will shortly reach its consummation in the return of Christ; and (6) an appeal for repentance for the forgiveness of sins.[56] Five of these elements of the kerygma are seen in Peter's sermon: the fulfillment of prophecy, the death and resurrection of Christ, the second advent, the offer of forgiveness, and the pouring out of the Holy Spirit on Cornelius and his household. Conversely, all these elements are captured in the preaching of Jesus.

Finally, there is the theme of the Holy Spirit. Liefeld is right to say that "if the narrative of Acts teaches theology at all, it teaches that the Holy Spirit is regularly active among God's people in this age."[57] The Gospel writers were emphatic about the role of the Holy Spirit in the ministry of Jesus. In this passage Peter says, "How God anointed Jesus of Nazareth with the Holy Spirit and power, who went around doing good and healing all who were oppressed by the devil, because God was with him" (10:38). The Holy Spirit was the source of Jesus's effective and empowered ministry. It is better echoed in the words of Gerald Hawthorne:

> By coming upon him, into him, at the baptism the Spirit anointed him with power and authority to carry out, fulfill, his mission as Messiah. By coming upon him, into him, the Spirit filled him to an even greater extent (if such it is possible) than he had filled him before, permeating his being, pervading his thinking, directing his steps, empowering him (cf. Luke 4:1–2). By coming upon him, the Spirit equipped him for service.[58]

If the Spirit was the cause of Jesus's powerful witnessing, then without the Holy Spirit there can be no ministry for the church. Luke portrays the Spirit as the one that commissioned Jesus as the Messiah of God, the apostles as first witnesses, and subsequent believers respectively.

---

56. Dodd, *Apostolic Preaching*, 21–23. For Bolt, the witnesses' speeches in Acts echo three necessities for the Christ: (1) to suffer; (2) to rise from the dead; and (3) for repentance looking to the forgiveness of sins to be proclaimed to the nations. See Bolt, "Mission and Witness," 197.

57. Liefeld, *Interpreting*, 84.

58. Hawthorne, *Presence and the Power*, 134.

## Conclusion: Implications for Preaching

What is left now is to deduce some implications for preaching by integrating the exegetical and theological themes in the passage. Some implications from the passage are similar to the ones that have already been posited in the previous chapters. Rather than looking at it as repetitive, it should be noted that these implications are from different witnesses. Also, this buttresses the point of this research that Spirit-empowered witnessing is demonstrated in mighty words and mighty works as seen in the life and ministry of Jesus. Thus, the similarities seen in all the chapters only validate the claim of this research because they are coming from different witnesses.

First, a Spirit-empowered witness is one who is sent to proclaim what they have seen and heard (Luke 24:48; John 15:27). In the passage, Peter testified that Jesus was sent to proclaim to the children of Israel the gospel of peace. The same can be said of Peter who was sent (having seen a vision and heard a voice) to the house of Cornelius (Acts 10:9–14). It was while he was wondering about the vision he had seen that the Spirit sent him on the mission to preach the gospel to Cornelius and his household (vv. 19–20). It should be noted that it was the Spirit that directed Peter into this mission; however, prior to the mission, Peter had seen a vision and heard from the Lord. In sum, a witness is one who proclaims what was heard and seen. Long states, "The witness has seen something, and the witness is willing to tell the truth about it – the whole truth and nothing but the truth."[59]

Therefore, a Spirit-empowered witness is bent on wrestling with the biblical text not merely gathering information about the text. Conscientious searching of the Scriptures and listening to the voice of the Spirit is mandatory if one is to speak with authority. This is why Jesus on many occasions asserts that he teaches and does what he has seen and heard from the Father (John 3:11; 5:19). It is through hearing and seeing from Scriptures that the preacher is able to speak with authority, which compels the audience to respond. Long states it well:

---

59. Long, *Witness of Preaching*, 47. Also, Fred B. Craddock echoes a similar view. He proposed that to preach, then, is to shout a whisper (i.e. to proclaim what we have heard, being true to the received tradition, but being careful to frame it in the context of the listeners). See Craddock, *Preaching*, 64.

> The preacher is listening for a voice, looking for a presence, hoping for the claim of God to be encountered through the text. Until this happens, there is nothing for the preacher to say. When it happens, the preacher becomes a witness to what has been seen and heard through the Scripture, and the preacher's authority grows out of this seeing and hearing.[60]

Indeed, the preacher is listening for a voice and looking for a presence in the text of Scripture. Thus, the preacher is called to a painstaking work of sermon preparation.

Second, Spirit-empowered witness is born out of prayer. Luke in Acts portrays the unflinching commitment of the apostles to the discipline of prayer as they followed in the steps of Jesus. He was consistent in emphasizing prayer in Acts as he did in his Gospel. Prayer was significant in the ministry of Jesus. As compared with other Gospels, Luke was the only one to note that Jesus was praying at the events of his baptism (Luke 3:21) and his transfiguration (Luke 9:29). Similarly in Acts, prayer was an integral practice of the believers, especially the apostles. In fact, the apostles were willing to forgo every other ministry commitment with the exception of the discipline of prayer and preaching the word. Peter says, "But we will devote ourselves to prayer and to the ministry of the word" (Acts 6:4). It was in keeping to this commitment to prayer that Peter saw a vision from the Lord that would lead to his sermon in the house of Cornelius (v. 9). Liefeld writes, "Prayer in Acts, then, was the means of accomplishing God's will and work. It was how one sought guidance."[61]

Therefore, it is imperative for a Spirit-empowered witness to practice the discipline of prayer. Of course, prayer is not an end to itself but it is one of the means of renewing grace. Also, it is a sign of total dependence on the Spirit, without which the witness is powerless. In prayer, the preacher expresses his insufficiency and need of divine grace to empower the person to witness. This is why Paul says, "Not that we are sufficient of ourselves to think any thing as of ourselves; but our sufficiency is of God" (2 Cor 3:5, KJV).

Third, a Spirit-empowered witness must be anointed with the Spirit. In chapter 2, the "anointing" was defined as empowerment to fulfill a divine

---

60. Long, *Witness of Preaching*, 47.
61. Liefeld, *Interpreting*, 88.

mandate. Peter says, "How God anointed Jesus of Nazareth with the Holy Spirit and power, who went around doing good and healing all who were oppressed by the devil, because God was with him" (v. 38). Jesus was filled with power by the Spirit to fulfill his messianic ministry. It was this infilling of the Holy Spirit that made all the difference in the life of Jesus. As Forbes would say, "The anointing makes the difference!"[62] The anointing of the Spirit was given to Jesus because he was always doing the will of the Father. At the baptism of Jesus, besides the Spirit descending upon him, the voice of God the Father testified that he was well-pleased with the Son (Luke 3:22). And Peter rightly said that the reason Jesus was able to do mighty works was because God was with him. Whether with Jesus in this passage, Joseph in Egypt (Acts 7:9), or the believers in Antioch (14:27), it is the presence of God in a witness that makes the difference. One unique thing about all these individuals was that they were sensitive to the Spirit of God in their lives. The conscious awareness of the presence of God in their lives made them pursue consecration.

Therefore, there is need for a witness to be sensitive and consecrated to the Spirit. Without daily consecration to the Spirit there can be no empowerment to do mighty works. It can be argued that Acts of the Apostles was intended to show that God is able to do remarkable things through people who yield themselves without reservation to the Spirit. Human strength and abilities fail woefully if one attempts to do ministry in the power of the flesh. Hawthorne cautions preachers against going into the ministry without the empowerment of the Spirit; he writes:

> Are you a minister of the Gospel or a teacher, intelligent, educated, learned in the Scriptures? The life of Jesus teaches that intelligence and learning are not in themselves sufficient when it comes to making God's message meaningful to those who hear it. It is the Spirit of God within the minister that makes the word a living word, sharper than any two-edged sword (Acts 2:4, 14–37, especially vv. 33 and 37).[63]

---

62. Forbes, *Holy Spirit & Preaching*, 16.
63. Hawthorne, *Presence and the Power*, 239.

The apostles in Acts are living proof of how preachers may exceed their human limitations. Despite their academic inadequacy, they were able to rise against all odds to fulfill their divinely-appointed mission.

Fourth, a Spirit-empowered witness is committed to presenting the gospel as a universal offer of salvation to all. Peter at his encounter with Cornelius realized that the gospel offer is to every creature under heaven, and that salvation is not only for a select few. Jesus preached that salvation is for "whosoever will." Undoubtedly, John 3:16 is the most popular verse in the entire Bible and it echoes the universal saving will of God and the universal offer of salvation. David L. Allen writes, "Without belief in the universal saving will of God and a universal extent in Christ's sin-bearing, there can be no well-meant offer of salvation from God to the non-elect who hear the gospel call."[64] In John 3:16, the purpose of God giving his only Son is so that whosoever will believe in him might be saved. God is a universal God; the atonement made by Christ is universal; everyone is entitled to hear the gospel; and everyone is commanded to respond in repentance and faith in Christ.

This realization was crucial, otherwise Peter would have been reluctant to preach to Cornelius and his household. R. Alan Streett, exposing the negative effect of some Calvinists who feel reluctant to offer a public invitation of the gospel, writes, "If Calvinist preachers, as well as others from different theological persuasions, would start calling their hearers to a public profession of faith, I believe the Holy Spirit would draw many more people to Christ under their ministry."[65] The Holy Spirit came to bear witness to Christ through human vessels. Hence, the Spirit will only empower those who are committed to crossing every form of human-made barriers to preach the gospel.

---

64. Allen, *Extent of the Atonement*, 786.

65. Streett, "Public Invitation and Calvinism," 252. Also, David L. Allen argued that "anything that operates to undermine the centrality, universality, and necessity of preaching is wrong. Anything that makes preachers hesitant to make the bold proclamation of the gospel to all people is wrong. Thinking that Christ only suffered for some will deeply affect preaching." See Allen, *Extent of the Atontement*, 98.

CHAPTER 6

# Conclusion: A Theology of Spirit-Empowered Witness

It has been observed in hermeneutics that in most cases, the problem is not with interpretation as much as it is with implications. E. D. Hirsch says, "Most of the practical problems of interpretation are problems of implication."[1] Interpreters tend to shift from the authorial intent of the text because of the implications it posits on one's theological belief. Despite this upheaval, one is still able to argue plausibly for some implications on the grounds of careful exegesis. Many implications have already been deduced in this research. The goal of this chapter is to harness all the exegetical results together in an organized pattern. This organization will answer the two research questions posited at the outset: (1) what does it mean to be Spirit-empowered? and (2) how can one seek the power of the Spirit in their preaching/teaching ministry? In a nutshell, it is addressing the "what" and "how" one can be Spirit-empowered to fulfill their ministry.[2]

---

1. Hirsch, *Validity in Interpretation*, 61.

2. We are affirming that the "what" and "how" of ministry should be modelled after the ministry of Jesus Christ. We are by no means implying that preachers today can equal or be compared to Jesus in ministry. No one will be able to be perfect like Jesus, but we are called to follow in his steps (1 Pet 2:21). J. Stuart Holden asserts that in the spiritual as in the natural world there is a law which declares that the same cause will, under the same conditions, produce the same consequences. Hence under the same conditions of surrender and dependence as in which our Lord lived his earthly life, the same cause – the eternal Spirit – will produce the same consequence, and our lives can thus be like his life (in kind though not in degree) in the reality and beauty of holiness. See Holden, *Price of Power*, 49.

## The Divine Cause

In order to present a theology of Spirit-empowered preaching, it is imperative for one to begin by definition. This research has argued that Spirit-empowered preaching is characterized by two marks: Spirit-word and Spirit-work. Therefore, Spirit-empowered preaching is an act of witnessing to Christ by a Spirit-empowered witness, which is accompanied by mighty words and mighty works. From Luke-Acts, we have investigated the ministry of Jesus Christ of Nazareth in order to establish this claim. Through an exegetical analysis of the testimonies of three witnesses, and the testimony of Jesus himself about his ministry, this definition was validated. A theology of Spirit-empowered preaching must be anchored and modeled after the ministry of Jesus Christ of Nazareth, who is the focus of preaching, and into whose image humanity seeks to be transformed (Rom 8:29). The overarching thrust of this research is that Jesus was mighty in words and works because God anointed him with the Holy Spirit and power. Without the empowerment of the Spirit, he would not have been able to fulfill his ministry. Hawthorne writes, "Jesus is living proof of how those who are his followers may exceed the limitations of their humanness in order that they, like him, might carry to completion against all odds their God-given mission in life – by the Holy Spirit."[3]

The Holy Spirit was the presence and power of God in the life of Jesus. He was the divine cause on which Jesus was dependent for his entire ministry. The Holy Spirit was what made the differences in the life and ministry of Jesus. According to John the Baptist, Jesus was filled with the Holy Spirit without measure (John 3:34). From the four testimonies investigated, one clause that captured the argument of this research was echoed in the speech of Peter. He says, "For God was with him" (Acts 10:38). How was God with Jesus? It was argued that God in the person of the Holy Spirit was with Jesus in at least three phases of his life:

First, the Holy Spirit was involved in Jesus's conception, birth, and infancy to prepare him. Jesus was conceived by the Spirit as the Son of God, and grew in wisdom and stature. As was argued in chapter 2, the baptism of Jesus was not the first experience of the Spirit in Jesus's life. Luke says, "The angel answered and said to her, 'The Holy Spirit will come upon you, and the power of the Most High will overshadow you; and for that reason the

---

3. Hawthorne, *Presence and the Power*, 234.

holy Child shall be called the Son of God'" (Luke 1:35). Hawthorne made a striking comment about this verse; he said, "The Holy Spirit of God who in the beginning was present in order to bring the first creation into existence (Gen 1:2) is the same Spirit who comes once again to bring the new creation into being in the conception of Jesus."[4] Thus, in Luke 1:35, the consequence of the work of the Holy Spirit in the conception and birth of Jesus is that Jesus would be called holy, and would be the Son of God. These two descriptions are crucial because they speak of his character.

Second, the Holy Spirit was at his commissioning to empower him. Dunn writes, "In view of the birth narratives of Matthew and Luke one can speak of Jesus' anointing with the Spirit at Jordan (Acts 10:38) as a second 'experience' of the Spirit."[5] At his baptism, Jesus was confirmed by God as his beloved Son and empowered (anointed) by the Spirit. Jesus said, "The Spirit of the Lord is upon me, because he has anointed me to proclaim good news to the poor, He has sent me to herald release to the captives and to the blind recovery of sight, to send in release to those oppressed, to herald the favorable year of the Lord" (Luke 4:18–19). Jesus was not the only one that affirmed this claim. Peter also testified to this as he said, "How God anointed Jesus of Nazareth with the Holy Spirit and power, who went around doing good and healing all who were oppressed by the devil, because God was with him" (Acts 10:38). He was anointed for his messianic mission, which implies that the Holy Spirit is the source or the means through which he would accomplish his mission. The nature of his mission is prophetic, which is "to herald release to the captives," through his mighty words and mighty works.

Third, the Holy Spirit was in his entire ministry to control and lead him. After his empowerment by the Spirit at the Jordan River, he was controlled entirely by the Spirit. In a striking manner, Luke portrays this principle in Jesus's life. Immediately after his baptism, Luke says, "Jesus, full of the Holy Spirit, returned from the Jordan and was led around by the Spirit in the wilderness" (Luke 4:1). In the wilderness, he through the Spirit was victorious over all the temptations of Satan. Thereafter, Luke says, "Jesus returned to Galilee in the power of the Spirit, and news about Him spread through all the surrounding district" (Luke 4:14). Then, after he accomplished his salvific

---

4. Hawthorne, 66.
5. Dunn, *Baptism in the Holy Spirit*, 23–24.

work and was raised from the dead, before his ascension, Luke says, "Until the day when he was taken up to heaven, after he had by the Holy Spirit given orders to the apostles whom he had chosen" (Acts 1:2). Thus, Jesus's entire ministry was led and controlled by the Spirit, which was the secret of his empowerment. Stephen F. Olford and David L. Olford believe that the secret of Jesus's anointing "is best summed up in three words: holiness, yieldedness, and prayerfulness."[6]

In sum, the life and ministry of Jesus Christ of Nazareth serves as a blueprint of the working of the Holy Spirit in a preacher. The Holy Spirit was the divine cause that prepared Jesus for the ministry from conception to adulthood. The Spirit came upon Mary, and caused her to conceive, and she gave birth to the eternal Son of God. Next, the Holy Spirit was the divine cause that came upon the eternal Son to empower him for his messianic ministry. Finally, the Holy Spirit was the divine cause that exerted absolute control of the life and ministry of the eternal Son. Therefore, these three phases of the divine cause are not optional if one is to experience the power of God in witnessing to Christ. Luke in Acts demonstrated how these three phases occurred in the apostles and disciples of Jesus. Since it was true for Jesus and his apostles, it implies that it will be true for anyone called to witness about Christ.

## The Divine Conditions for Empowerment

Unconditional election as affirmed by Calvinists has caused many Christians to be wary of statements that assert certain conditions. It is clear in the Gospels that Jesus pronounced many profound truths using conditional statements.[7]

---

6. Olford and Olford, *Anointed Expository Preaching*, 218. Interestingly, all the three words that the Olfords proposed from the life of Jesus were all deduced from Luke 3:21–22. They noted that God only blesses with the anointing of his Holy Spirit those who pursue a life of holiness. They also asserted that we must initially obey the gospel to know the gift of the Spirit; but we must continually obey to know the fullness and anointing of the Spirit. With holiness and obedience, they insist that a life of prayerfulness is not only initial, but also continuous. This is where we begin, and when we receive the Holy Spirit at first, we are born again; however, the prayer-life is the life that is always seeking and always receiving – the filling, the infilling and overflowing of the Spirit. Olford and Olford, 218–19.

7. When speaking about the new birth, Jesus says to Nicodemus, "Truly, truly, I say to you, unless one is born of water and the Spirit he cannot enter into the kingdom of God" (John 3:5). When speaking about the infilling of the Spirit he says to the people, "If anyone

Rejecting conditional statements is tantamount to rejecting the teachings of Christ and the Spirit. The empowerment of the Spirit is a free gift to all, but it must be received. Hawthorne says, "All, however, must receive the Holy Spirit on their own, by their own choice."[8] The Spirit did not infringe upon or force Jesus's freedom. Similarly, the Spirit does not overpower a person's free choice. Every preacher has the choice to receive the empowerment of the Spirit or not – to be led by the Spirit or not. However, if one desires to be empowered by the Spirit, then there are conditions to be met. These conditions are all drawn from the implications deduced from the exegetical work. In order to avoid legalism, it is worth noting that all these conditions are made possible through the merits of the redemptive work of Jesus, not because of a person's piety.

## There Must Be a Conversion Experience

There are three calls a witness receives in the biblical sense: a call to salvation, a call to holiness, and a call to service.[9] The call to service is not the first call an individual receives from God. God issues the call to salvation first, then the call to holiness, and finally the call to service. God is first interested in the private life of a witness before their public life. Stott calls it the personal experience of Jesus Christ, which is the first indispensable mark of the Christian witness because they cannot speak from hearsay; they must be able to speak from their own experience.[10] Conversion comes before commission. In conversion, the witness experiences the Holy Spirit for the first time. The word of God is preached, and the Spirit uses the word to convict a person of sin and of the need for a savior. Through repentance and faith, the witness receives forgiveness of sins and the gift of the indwelling Spirit.

---

is thirsty, let him come to me and drink" (John 7:37). When speaking about discipleship he says, "If anyone wishes to come after me, he must deny himself, and take up his cross daily and follow me" (Luke 9:23). In fact, the book of Revelation concludes with the Spirit and the church using conditional statements to call people, "The Spirit and the bride say, 'Come.' And let the one who hears say, 'Come.' And let the one who is thirsty come; let the one who wishes take the water of life without cost" (Rev 22:17).

8. Hawthorne, *Presence and the Power*, 236.

9. Prime and Begg, *Being a Pastor*, 20. Prime and Begg argued for this view from 1 Corinthians 1:1–9: call to fellowship (v. 9); call to holiness (v. 2); and a call to service (v. 1).

10. Stott, *Preacher's Portrait*, 71.

Jesus did not need to repent of sin, as Matthew's account indicated by John the Baptist's reluctance to baptize Jesus at first; however, Jesus insisted on going through the ceremony to fulfill all righteousness (Matt 3:14–15). According to Dunn, "the baptism of John was not a repentance baptism, resulting in the forgiveness of sins, but rather an expression of the repentance which results in the forgiveness of sins (Acts 3:19; 5:31; 10:43; 11:18; 13:38; 26:18)."[11] Although not a sinner, Jesus identified with the nation of Israel by submitting to the baptism of John, which expressed repentance from sin and faith towards God. On the other hand, at Pentecost and thereafter, the disciples of Jesus were baptized after they repented of their sins. When Peter preached on the day of Pentecost, Luke says the people were "pierced to the heart" and asked Peter what they must do to be saved (Acts 2:37). The "piercing to the heart" is also known as conviction, which only the Holy Spirit can perform (John 16:8). Peter then said to them, "Repent, and each of you be baptized in the name of Jesus Christ for the forgiveness of your sins; and you will receive the gift of the Holy Spirit" (Acts 2:38). The gift of the Spirit is what is also called the baptism of the Spirit, for all believers have been baptized by one Spirit (1 Cor 12:13). Heisler writes, "This initial experience of the Spirit's work of regeneration within us is powerful because it marks us for life. We cannot approach preaching without it."[12] In order to bear witness to Christ, one must be a witness.

## There Must Be a Pursuit of Holiness

Second to the call to salvation is the call to holiness. After conversion has taken place in an individual, the Spirit then begins the work of character development. A person enters a sonship relationship with God, which can be confirmed by the reception of the Spirit. Paul says, "Because you are sons, God

---

11. Dunn, *Baptism in the Holy Spirit*, 15. Dunn notes that John's baptism was essentially preparatory, not initiatory, a prophetic symbol of the messianic baptism, in that it symbolized and prepared the way for the action and experience of the messianic judgment. In its immediate application as a rite it proclaimed God's willingness to cleanse the penitent there and then and to bring him safely through the coming wrath. Like the rites of the Old Testament, it enabled the repentant person to draw near to God by giving him a visible expression of his repentance and a symbol of God's forgiveness. By nurturing the repentance and bringing it to full flower the baptism provided the occasion for the divine-human encounter in which the forgiveness was received. Dunn, 17.

12. Heisler, *Spirit-Led Preaching*, 69.

has sent forth the Spirit of His Son into our hearts, crying, 'Abba! Father!'" (Gal 4:6). The Holy Spirit comes to take his residence in a believer to begin the work of sanctification. Stott asserts that the Spirit comes both to reveal Christ to us and to form Christ in us, so that we grow steadily in our knowledge of Christ and in the likeness of Christ (Eph 1:17; Gal 4:19; 2 Cor 3:18).[13] It is through the power of the indwelling Spirit that evil desires and worldly lusts are restrained, while the fruit of the Spirit strives in the character of the believer. In a nutshell, "the chief work of the Holy Spirit is to make believers holy, and the truest evidence of the exertion of His power in any life is seen in the realm of character."[14]

It was stated explicitly in chapter 2 that Jesus absolutely surrendered to the Spirit. Luke affirmed that Jesus was born of the Holy Spirit and he lived a holy life all through his earthly ministry. In fact, not even the hostile Jews could convict Jesus of sin (John 8:46). The Holy Spirit empowerment necessitates a relinquishment of besetting sins and a life of purity. Holden says, "A great difficulty with many is that they want power without purity, and happiness without holiness."[15] Preachers are channels or agents through whom the Spirit testifies to Christ; Paul made it clear that only holy vessels will be used for noble purposes (2 Tim 2:21). Undoubtedly, the path of consecration to holiness is a painstaking one, and few are willing to renounce the self-life to walk the narrow road of holiness. Commenting on holiness, Stott says, "I cannot help wondering if this may not be why there are so few preachers whom God is using today. There are plenty of popular preachers, but not many powerful ones, who preach in the power of the Spirit. Is it because the cost of such preaching is too great?"[16] Indeed, the cost is great, but no one is called to walk that path alone. Only through the grace of God, which is revealed in Christ through the power of the Spirit, is a preacher able to walk that path.

Holiness is impossible with humans. A man may try by willpower to achieve holiness, but it would not be long before the person realizes the impossibility. Arguably in Romans 7, Paul laments his daily struggle with

---

13. Stott, *Baptism and Fullness*, 20.
14. Holden, *Price of Power*, 63.
15. Holden, 70.
16. Stott, *Preacher's Portrait*, 122. According to Stott, there are two essential conditions to receiving the power of the Holy Spirit: holiness and humility. Stott, 120.

indwelling sin.[17] The things he detests, he finds himself doing, and the things he desires to do, he does not do. The more he tries, the more he recedes further into the realm of impossibility, which leads to his cry of despair, "Wretched man that I am! Who will set me free from the body of this death?" (Rom 7:24). John Owen the Puritan preacher writes, "Mortification of any sin must be by a supply of grace. Of ourselves we cannot do it."[18] Paul found his deliverance in Christ, who through the Spirit set him free from the law of sin and death (Rom 8:2). Such is the case for every Christian; it is only through the power of the indwelling Spirit that one is able to mortify sin and to live in purity (Rom 8:13).

Thus, it is through dependence on the Spirit that renunciation of sin and self becomes a reality. Owen writes, "The Spirit is the author and finisher of our sanctification; gives new supplies and influences of grace for holiness and sanctification, when the contrary principle is weakened and abated (Eph. 3:16–18)."[19] This dying to self and sin is through an absolute surrender to the revealed will of God in the Scriptures. That is, obedience to the voice of the Holy Spirit in Scriptures and the voice within the believer (Acts 5:32). In the Scriptures, believers are called to die daily to sin and self (Luke 9:23–24; 1 Cor 15:31). Owen writes, "Do you mortify; do you make it your daily work; be always at it while you live; be killing sin or it will be killing you."[20]

---

17. Romans 7, especially verses 13–25, is a controversial paragraph due to the diversity of interpretations in scholarship. Some scholars like Douglas J. Moo believe that Paul was making reference to his unregenerate state. See Moo, *Epistle to the Romans*, 443–51. On the other hand, scholars like Robert H. Mounce, Leon Morris, James D. G. Dunn, and Charles Cranfield believe Paul was referring to his regenerate state of struggle with indwelling sin. See Mounce, *Romans*, 166–67; Morris, *Epistle to the Romans*, 290; Dunn, *Romans 1–8*, 403–12; Cranfield, *Critical and Exegetical Commentary*, 355–56. Yet, there is another group like J. C. O'Neill who deny that Paul wrote the paragraph. See O'Neill, *Paul's Letter*, 131. In view of the larger context, which is dealing with sanctification, we affirm the regenerate position.

18. Owen, *Overcoming Sin and Temptation*, 133.

19. Owen, 139.

20. Owen, 50. Also, Yancey Arrington in his book *Tap: Defeating the Sins that Defeat You* asserts that there are three responses to sin by believers. The first is the discount response. This is a person that "knows he shouldn't do certain things but it's really not that big of a deal. Sin is viewed like a bothersome fly that harmlessly buzzes around. And because it is only bothersome but not dangerous, the person takes a 'wink, wink' mentality to sin." The second is the surrender response. "This is the person who has tried to battle a sin here and there but failed at it so miserably that they have given up. In other words, they've tapped out." Finally, the third approach is the fight response. This person is "neither discounting sin's importance nor surrendering himself to sin's power, but instead he views the struggle with sin as a very real fight – a fight that is winnable!" See Arrington, *Tap*, 25–26.

## There Must Be a Call to Service

After the call to salvation and holiness, the next call to all Christians is the call to service. Thus, all Christians are expected to be fruitful in the kingdom of God. However, within the universal call of service to all Christians, there is a call to some Christians to engage their entire lives to the proclamation of the gospel. Jeff Iorg says, "All believers are called to Christian service, but God calls some believers to ministry leadership."[21] It is to this group that this research is geared, those called to the full-time preaching/teaching ministry. The caution of Spurgeon is needed more today than in his time. He lamented about the decadence he saw in the ministry in his day,

> That hundreds have missed their way, and stumbled against a pulpit is sorrowfully evident from the fruitless ministries and decaying churches which surround us. It is a fearful calamity to a man to miss his calling, and to the church upon whom he imposes himself, his mistake involves an affliction of the most grievous kind.[22]

Jesus did not stumble into ministry on his own volition. God sent him, and in that same way Jesus sent his disciples.[23] It was because God sent him that the Holy Spirit anointed him. Jesus said in his Nazareth sermon (see chapter 2) that he was sent to herald emancipation to the captives. Similarly, after his resurrection he sent his disciples on a mission to testify about the kingdom of God by empowering them with the Spirit. Thus, only those who are

---

21. Iorg, *Is God Calling Me?*, 24. Also, Iorg asserts that there are three types of calling experiences: the universal call to Christian service and growth; a general call to ministry leadership; and a specific call to a ministry assignment. As to the specific call to ministry, he sees it as an additional call experience made to those who are called to ministry leadership position; however, it is to a specific task. Iorg, 17–29.

22. Spurgeon, *Lectures to My Students*, 26.

23. Jesus was commissioned and empowered by the Father at the Jordan River to carry out his mission. In similar fashion, he commissioned and sent out his disciples. After the resurrection of Jesus, he appeared to his disciples and gave them specific instructions for their mission. On one occasion he came and said, "Peace be with you; as the Father has sent me, I also send you" (John 20:21). On another occasion he said, "But you will receive power when the Holy Spirit has come upon you; and you shall be my witnesses both in Jerusalem, and in all Judea and Samaria, and even to the remotest part of the earth" (Acts 1:8). In this verse he tells them the means of their commission, what their mission is, and the locations where he is sending them on mission. These two verses were the foundational thrust to the disciples and remain so to all Christians today, especially those called into the ministry. In addition, they presume some conditions to be gratified.

called into the ministry are going to be empowered for the specific task. The Holy Spirit's empowerment is the power to do the will of God. The Scripture teaches clearly that the Holy Spirit appoints and empowers some individuals for specific service in the Christian ministry. In Acts 13:1–3, the Holy Spirit explicitly instructed the church at Antioch to set aside Saul (Paul) and Barnabas for the work to which he called them. The Holy Spirit is the one that calls certain individuals to specific service.

Some have entered the ministry more from their own desire rather than from the call of God on their lives. J. H. Jowett describes this group of individuals as having a personal calculation, or from the secular counsel of friends.[24] This is where a man takes up the ministry as a profession, as a means of earning a living, as a desirable social distinction, and due to his coveting of a leadership position. The constraining motive for a person with a horizontal vision is ambition and the coveted goal is success.[25] To enter the ministry because of a horizontal vision is to underestimate the exigencies and the demands of the ministry. It is to equate the ministry among secular alternatives that one can choose due to personal appeal.

In contrast to the horizontal vision, there is the vertical vision. This is where the conviction comes from the eternal God. Jowett describes the call of God in a startling way:

> The call of the Eternal must ring through the rooms of his soul as clearly as the sound of the morning-bell rings through the valleys of Switzerland, calling the peasants to early prayer and praise. The candidate for the ministry must move like a man in secret bonds. "Necessity is laid" upon him.[26]

This call gives the preacher no other option; there are no alternatives for them to choose. Also, no man can describe for another how the divine call comes because, as seen in Scripture, God calls people differently. The call of Amos was different from that of Isaiah, Moses, and Paul. Every call is unique, and thus one person cannot tell the manner of its coming to another person. In spite of the uniqueness of the divine call, and the reality that no one can

---

24. Jowett, *Preacher*, 11.
25. Jowett, 12.
26. Jowett, 12.

describe to another how the call will come to them, every preacher must have two confirmations to their call to ministry traditionally speaking: the inward call and the outward call. According to Derek Prime and Alistair Begg, in the inward call an individual becomes personally aware of their calling through their encounter with God. The outward call is where God's people recognize the calling and gifts an individual has for the ministry.[27]

Therefore, the call to ministry must come from above, and then the church should validate the call. Charles Bridges noted that "one of the causes of ministerial failure can sometimes be traced to the threshold of the entrance into the work because the promise of God is assured only where the call is manifest."[28] What happens if a person goes without the call? Simply put, there will not be empowerment from the Spirit for that particular task. This is not because their doctrine was unsound, but that they preached unsent.[29] The assurance of being sent is foundational to the preaching ministry. Paul says, "How will they preach unless they are sent? Just as it is written, 'How beautiful are the feet of those who bring Good News of good things'" (Rom 10:15). Consequently, one must not forget the key factor that it is God the Holy Spirit that issues the call.[30] The call comes through sensitivity to the Spirit's dealing with us as we engage in prayer, read the word, and listen to the preaching of the word.

## There Must Be Preparation for Service

John R. Bisagno says, "A call to preach is a call to preparation. A call to serve is a call to prepare to serve."[31] He went on to review the life of Moses, Paul, and Jesus to emphasize the need of preparation. Bisagno noted that though Moses was well learned in secular culture of Egypt, he later had to unlearn

---

27. Prime and Begg, *Being a Pastor*, 24. Also, Charles Bridges calls the two calls: the internal call and the external call. See Bridges, *Christian Ministry*, 91. Spurgeon sees four confirmatory signs of one who is called to the ministry. First, there must be a heavenly calling, which is an intense, all-absorbing desire for the work. Second there must be aptness to teach and some measure of the other qualities needful for the office of a public instructor. Third, a person must see a measure of conversion-work going on under his efforts. Finally, there must be the prayerful judgment of the person's church (i.e. one's preaching should be acceptable to the people of God). See Spurgeon, *Lectures to My Students*, 27–34.

28. Bridges, *Christian Ministry*, 90.
29. Bridges, 90.
30. Prime and Begg, *Being a Pastor*, 22.
31. Bisagno, *Letters to Timothy*, 39.

much of what he had learned. He writes, "He [Moses] had to learn to depend on what God would teach him more than what men could teach him. So, it was off to the backside of the desert for forty years. There he tended sheep and learned to wait on God."[32] The lives of Moses, the apostles, and Jesus clearly teach that intelligence and learning are not in themselves sufficient when it comes to proclaiming the gospel. This is not to say that secular or theological training is not important. Whether one gets a theological training or not is by no means the focus of this section.[33] The point is that God desires spiritual things to be done in the Spirit, not by solely depending on natural abilities. Therefore, a preacher needs to learn how to depend on the Holy Spirit rather than on his own skills. God said to Zerubbabel, "Not by might nor by power, but by My Spirit,' says the LORD of hosts" (Zech 4:6).

Luke emphasized the dependence on the Spirit and learning attitude of Jesus in his gospel. Jesus was presented as one who depended on the Spirit and thus grew in wisdom and stature prior to his ministry (Luke 2:52). When he was twelve years old, his parents went to Jerusalem for the feast of the Passover. On their way back to Nazareth they discovered he was missing. They returned to Jerusalem and found him after three days in the temple, conversing with the teachers. Luke says, "And all who heard Him were amazed at his understanding and his answers" (Luke 2:47). Forbes noted that this account of Jesus engaging with the teachers in the temple reflects his keen interest in learning from those who were masters of the tradition.[34] Furthermore, in chapter 4 of this work, it was stated that after his resurrection, Jesus continued through the Holy Spirit to give instructions to his disciples. Jesus in his life and ministry taught the disciples the importance on depending on the Holy Spirit. Thus, it was after Jesus had finished his years of preparation that he was commissioned and empowered. He became a teacher who came from

---

32. Bisagno, 39.

33. Although not making a case for formal education, I hold that theological training is important. Bisagno's advice should be noted,

> By all means, do everything possible to secure a seminary education. But if that opportunity eludes your grasp, seek God with all your heart, serve him in the beauty of holiness, be faithful to every opportunity, and he will still use you in a wonderful way . . . Good preparation does not ensure great usability. But the chances of great usability are severely limited when formal education is lacking.

See Bisagno, 40–41.

34. Forbes, *Holy Spirit & Preaching*, 32.

God with a word from God. Stott says, "If, then, we would bear witness to Jesus we shall be found constantly with the Bible in our hand, for it is there that the Father's testimony to the Son is to be found."[35]

Luke also wrote of the apostles' learning at the feet of Jesus for three years. After Jesus's ascension, they continued learning the discipline of waiting on the Spirit. O'Reilly writes, "The time before the coming of the Spirit is a time for waiting and for prayer, a time to realize that without the Spirit the followers of Jesus can quite literally do nothing to implement the mission which he had entrusted to them."[36] On the tenth day of waiting, Jesus poured out his Spirit upon his disciples on the day of Pentecost and they were filled with the Spirit and went about preaching with great power. Their preaching and miracles were so astonishing that the rulers, elders, and scribes in Jerusalem wanted to know the source of their power and learning. Luke says, "Now as they observed the confidence of Peter and John and understood that they were uneducated and untrained men, they were amazed, and began to recognize them as having been with Jesus" (Acts 4:13).

The mystery of the mighty words and mighty works of the apostles is their learning at the feet of Jesus. They learned to depend on the teachings of Christ and on the power of the Holy Spirit. Similarly, Paul emphasized to the churches at Corinth and Thessalonica that his entire preaching was not with the wisdom of men's words but his dependence on the demonstration of the power of the Spirit (1 Cor 2:4; 1 Thess 1:5). He was not advocating negligence in careful preparation; rather, he was arguing that the object of his confidence is the power of the Spirit and not his fluent speech. In describing a preacher who is confident in his ability to entice people, Stott believes that the preacher "may certainly succeed in swaying their emotions and arousing them to action of some kind, but the work will be neither deep nor lasting."[37]

The Holy Spirit prepares the preacher through the act of spiritual disciplines such as prayer, meditation, fasting, etc. These disciplines strip off self-confidence and teach dependence on the Spirit. God is interested in preachers who will saturate their minds with the word because the word sanctifies the

---

35. Stott, *Preacher's Portrait*, 67.
36. O'Reilly, *Word and Sign*, 15–16.
37. Stott, *Preacher's Portrait*, 117.

preacher. They not only linger in the word, they also memorize Scriptures, live in obedience to the word, and are committed to prayer. Holden writes,

> Part of the price of power is time spent in secret communion with God. Those who will not take time for the study of the Word of God and for prayer, will never know the fullness of His power working through them. It is only by maintaining the attitude of waiting in His presence, that we can learn to know ourselves and to know Him, and seeing the things of our lives in His light can judge them by His standards. All our public life before men is at its best a reflection and echo of our private life before God.[38]

This statement is true of the apostles. They were prepared for ministry in the school of spiritual formation, which taught them how to balance their public life and private life. E. M. Bounds writes, "The preacher is commissioned to pray as well as to preach. His mission is incomplete if he does not do both well."[39] The apostles were men of prayer and great preachers. They were willing to relinquish all other good services to devote themselves to the preaching of the word and prayer (Acts 6:2–4). Heisler says, "Preaching is not so much about you preparing a sermon to preach; preaching is about God preparing you – his vessel – to preach."[40] Therefore, only through the Holy Spirit's preparation can a preacher's word engage the mind, enflame the heart, and move the will to action.

---

38. Holden, *Price of Power*, 14–15.
39. Bounds, *Power Through Prayer*, 39.
40. Heisler, *Spirit-Led Preaching*, 15. Similarly, Stott says,

> There is no greater need for the preacher than that he should know God. I care not about his lack of eloquence and artistry, about his ill-constructed discourse or his poorly enunciated message, if only it is evident that God is a reality to him and the he has learned to abide in Christ. The preparation of the heart is of far greater importance than the preparation of the sermon. The preacher's words, however clear and forceful, will not ring true unless he speaks from conviction born of experience. Many sermons, which conform to all the best homiletical rules, yet have a hollow sound. There is something indefinably perfunctory about the preacher of such sermons. The matter of his sermon gives evidence of a well-stocked, well-disciplined mind; he has a good voice, a fine bearing, and restrained gestures, but somehow his heart is not in his message.

See Stott, *Preacher's Portrait*, 76.

## There Must Be a Commitment to Christocentric Mission

In Jesus's manifesto in Nazareth, Luke depicts the inclusion of the Gentiles (2:30–32; 3:6) in God's plan of salvation. It was stated in chapter 2 that the overarching picture is that God desires to save all, not only the chosen race of Israel. It is a global rescue plan that God has undertaken to accomplish through the Messiah. Peter came to this realization in the house of Cornelius, and he confessed that now he knows that God does not show partiality; God accepts people from every nation who fear him and are willing to do his will (Acts 10:34–35). What then is the nature of this global mission? The one clause that captures the nature of Jesus's global ministry is "to herald release to the captives" (Luke 4:18b). This release was accomplished through his preaching theme of the kingdom of God.

As defined in chapter 4, the kingdom of God is the rule of God in the works and person of Christ. When John the Baptist was in prison, he sent two of his disciples to ask Jesus if he was the Christ (Luke 7:18–20). Jesus simply said to them, "Go and report to John what you have seen and heard: the blind receive sight, the lame walk, the lepers are cleansed, and the deaf hear, the dead are raised up, the poor have the Gospel preached to them" (Luke 7:22). Amidst the mighty works mentioned to John's disciples, Jesus spoke of the preaching of the gospel as a sign of his ministry. The gospel was central to Jesus. It is to the centrality of the gospel that Stott says, "It came from God and centered on Christ. God was its author, and Christ its substance."[41]

In the testimony of the two disciples walking to Emmaus (Luke 24:13–35), Jesus confronted them with an exposition of the gospel in the Old Testament. He told them that what had happened to him was a fulfillment of the Scriptures, for the Old Testament prophets foretold of the suffering, death, burial, and resurrection of the Messiah. Also, Luke testified that after Jesus was raised from the dead, he appeared to the disciples and apostles for forty days, speaking things about the kingdom of God (Acts 1:3). Similarly, it was argued in chapter 5 that the apostolic preaching was focused on the theme of the kingdom of God. In the house of Cornelius, Peter presented the gospel, which was christological in focus. It was the gospel of God's grace to all people in the person of Jesus Christ.

---

41. Stott, *Preacher's Portrait*, 116–17.

The Spirit's desire is to fill the earth with the knowledge of the glory of God reflected in the face of Christ. Therefore, the Spirit calls preachers to embark in a global mission of the universal offer of salvation through the proclamation of the gospel. The Spirit sent Peter, a Jew, to preach Christ to Cornelius, a Gentile (Acts 10). The Spirit directed Philip to preach to the Samaritans and later to an Ethiopian eunuch (Acts 8). Also, the Spirit called and sent Paul and Barnabas to preach to the Gentiles (Acts 13). Jesus said to his disciples, "When the Helper comes, whom I will send to you from the Father, that is the Spirit of truth who proceeds from the Father, He will testify about Me" (John 15:26).

Therefore, preachers are called to witness to Christ wherever the Spirit sends them regardless of ethnicity or cultural barriers. It is in the preaching of the cross of Christ that one encounters the power of God (1 Cor 1:23–24). Unless one is ready to testify about the teaching and works of Jesus, the Spirit will not empower the message. Any motive other than to glorify Christ will not attract the blessings of the Spirit. Holden noted that one of the most powerful hindrances for the power of the Holy Spirit on a preacher is impure motives. He writes,

> Others wish for great preaching power, the ability to become "front rank men," the magnetic influence to draw crowds to their ministry, or the reputation which will secure for them high place in church and world. And hence these "ask and have not" because they would indeed "consume it upon their lusts." . . . But the Holy Spirit is given solely for the glory of Jesus in the life and service of His disciples, and not for any glory or merely personal benefit to them.[42]

Christ is the focus of preaching, and the Holy Spirit came to reveal Christ to the world. The goal of preaching is that people would see the glory of God revealed in Christ, and thus be transformed into the image of Christ.

## There Must Be a Desire to Be Empowered

One implication that was deduced in chapter 4 is that the witness needs to be filled with the power of the Spirit. To be clear, the filling with the power

---

42. Holden, *Price of Power*, 72.

of the Spirit here is referring to the empowerment for preaching.[43] For one to be empowered with the power of the Spirit, there must be a desire. One reason many preachers do not desire the power of the Spirit is because they are unwilling to concede that they are void of power; they assume they have it so why should they desire something they already have. Stott says, "The first step towards such enduement with the power is the humble acknowledgement of our lack of it."[44] To be sure, the disciples were already converted and received the Spirit prior to Pentecost (John 20:22); however, they waited in anticipation of the empowerment of the Spirit. They eagerly desired the empowerment of the Holy Spirit and were praying with one mind and heart (Acts 1:14; 2:1). Without a true desire of the power of the Spirit, there will be no reception. Jesus said, "Blessed are those who hunger and thirst for righteousness, for they shall be satisfied" (Matt 5:6). This is a promise made by Christ to all those seeking to be filled with righteousness. He goes on to affirm that the promise will be fulfilled because it seeks to glorify God. The

---

43. To be filled with the Spirit is a heritage of every Christian (Eph 5:18). In fact, Jesus gave an open invitation to whosoever desires to experience the overflowing life of the Spirit to come to him (John 7:37–39). However, as has been argued in this research, Luke reserves the expression "filled with" or "full of the Holy Spirit" primarily for inspired witness about Jesus or against the devil. This view has been accepted and argued by many Lukan scholars. See Shelton, *Mighty in Word*, 136–48; O'Reilly, *Word and Sign*, 44–49; Menzies, *Empowered for Witness*, 174–201. Thus, this should not be assumed as a contradiction; rather, it calls for careful study of the Scriptures. Stott compared the various New Testament texts which speak of people being "filled with" or "full of" the Holy Spirit and concluded that there are three main categories. According to Stott, the first category was a normal characteristic of every dedicated Christian; the second category indicates an endowment for a particular ministry or office; and the third category was an equipping by the Spirit not so much for lifelong office, but for an immediate task, especially in an emergency. Stott, *Baptism & Fullness*, 48–49. The filling of the Spirit in this work is referring to the second category.

44. Stott, *Baptism & Fullness*, 106. Stott writes,

> the churches are busy using statistics to pull the wool over their own eyes. We seem unwilling to admit the grievously weak state of the Church today. We are content to judge with man's judgment, and to look on outward appearances only. Consequently, we do not see the worldliness of the Church, the lack of conviction of sin and of a vision of God, the externalism of much of our worship, the shallowness of our fellowship, our disobedience in the matter of evangelism, and the poor approximation of our lives to the standard of meekness and holiness set before us in the Beatitudes. We need power not only in our lives, but also in our ministry. As preachers we shall never begin to seek the power of God until we have come to see the futility of attempting to proclaim God's word in man's weakness alone."

Stott, 106.

same can be said of the power of the Spirit. In fact, Paul told the Corinthians to desire the gifts of the Spirit, including empowerment (1 Cor 14:1).

A desperate desire for the power of the Spirit leads one to desperate seeking. David says, "O God, you are my God; I shall seek you earnestly; my soul thirsts for you, my flesh yearns for you, in a dry and weary land where there is no water. Thus I have seen you in the sanctuary, to see your power and your glory" (Ps 63:1–2). This desire is manifested in the seeker's daily prayer, which is a demonstration of faith without which nothing is received from God (Heb 11:6). Luke says, "Now when all the people were baptized, Jesus was also baptized, and while he was praying, heaven was opened, and the Holy Spirit descended upon him in bodily form like a dove, and a voice came out of heaven, 'You are My beloved Son, in You I am well-pleased'" (Luke 3:21–22). It was while Jesus was praying that he was empowered by the Spirit. The same was recorded about the apostles in the day of Pentecost, they were praying and waiting in one accord when the Spirit came upon them (Acts 1:14; 2:1). It is clear that the empowerment is received in prayer, which is in the name of Jesus. Through a prayer of faith, the preacher is able to appropriate the power of the Spirit in his life to fulfill his ministry (Luke 11:9–13; Jas 1:5–8). Holden's advice is worth noting, "Much prayer means much power; little prayer means little power; no prayer means no power."[45]

The empowerment of the Spirit is not intended to be a one-time experience. It was pointed out in chapter 4 that there is the need for continuous infilling of the Spirit as seen in the book of Acts. Although the disciples were empowered on the day of Pentecost in Acts 2, Luke noted in Acts 4 how the

---

45. Holden, *Price of Power*, 15. Bridges asserts that without prayer, a minister is of no use to the church, nor of any advantage to mankind.

> He sows; and God gives no increase. He preaches; and his words are only like "sounding brass, or tinkling cymbal." He recites the praises of God; while "his heart is far from Him." It is prayer alone, then that gives the whole strength and efficacy to our different administrations: and that man ceases, if I may use the expression, to be a public minister from the time he ceases to pray. It is prayer, which supplies him with consolation in all his labors; and he celebrates the ordinances of religion, as the hireling performs his work – he considers them as a heavy task, or a severe imposition, if prayer doth not assuage its troubles, or console him for want of success . . . Prayer therefore is one half of our ministry; and it gives to the other half all its power and success. It is the appointed medium of receiving spiritual communications for the instruction of our people.

See Bridges, *Christian Ministry*, 147–48.

disciples prayed for more infilling of the Spirit. This is important because one needs to maintain a constant inflow and outflow of the Spirit in his ministry. For this to happen, Jesus taught his disciples that they would need to come to him daily (John 7:37–39). The continuous coming to him daily to appropriate the fullness of the Spirit is an act of faith, dependence, and obedience. Jerry Vines and Jim Shaddix believe that "the anointing must be sought day by day in the pastor's walk with God, in his preparation process, and in each individual preaching event."[46] Also, it is by coming daily to be filled with the Spirit that the Spirit displaces the self-life in us as well. Holden writes,

> We are only self-emptied by being Spirit-filled . . . What is required as the price of power, however, is a willingness to be emptied, and then in the enablement of the Spirit a continuous looking away from self, – even from the thus emptied self, and a looking off unto Jesus, who increasingly becomes to us, by the guidance and teaching of the Comforter, Lord and King.[47]

An unsanctified ambition to be filled with the power of the Spirit for personal glorification will not be honored. The power of the Spirit is for doing the will of the Father, not one's selfish desire. Hawthorne says, "The Holy Spirit is God present and active in the lives of Jesus's followers, not to make life rich and comfortable for them, but to equip them to fulfill God's mission for them in the world."[48] The power of the Spirit is to witness to Christ. One should not expect the power of the Holy Spirit unless one is appointed or called by the Spirit into the work for which one is seeking power even if the desire is genuine. This is because the Spirit has the prerogative to separate and send those whom he chooses for service (Acts 13:2–4). Also, it was pointed out in chapter 4 that the power of the Spirit can be lost or quenched, as indicated in the Scriptures (Luke 9:37–45; 1 Thess 5:19). There are many reasons, which are

---

46. Vines and Shaddix, *Power in the Pulpit*, 66.
47. Holden, *Price of Power*, 85.
48. Hawthorne, *Presence and the Power*, 243. Similarly, Holden noted that God does not invest a man with power for any other work than that of the kingdom, and no man who does not renounce all forms of leadership other than the spiritual can ever know the enduement of a personal Pentecost. Politics, literature, and fine arts, intellectual pursuits, etc., have each their own legitimate sphere, but the power of the Holy Spirit is never bestowed to make a man a worker or a leader in these things. Only for the glory of Christ in the salvation of souls can the holy anointing be sought with any certainty of realization; and herein is the explanation of the failure of much desire and many prayers. See Holden, *Price of Power*, 13.

impossible to list exhaustively; however, quenching the Spirit can be avoided by walking daily in the Spirit. This daily walk in the Spirit involves coming to Jesus daily through faith, obedience, and dependence.

## The Divine Consequences

This research has argued exegetically from the ministry of Jesus that Spirit-empowered preaching is characterized by two marks, namely, Spirit-words and Spirit-works. These two are complementary of each other; thus, there cannot be one without the other. Jesus was a prophet mighty in both words and works. The Holy Spirit was the source or means of the powerful words and works of the eternal Son. Therefore, this section is simply asserting that under the same conditions of conversion, holiness, call to service, preparation for service, Christocentric focus, and desperate seeking, the same Holy Spirit (divine cause) will produce the same consequences.

### Jesus Mighty in Words and Works

Luke and the entire synoptic tradition attest to the powerful preaching and healing of Jesus. People were astonished at his preaching and miracles, and wondered where he got his power and authority (Matt 13:54). In fact, it was said that his preaching was not like the scribes (Matt 7:29; Mark 1:22). Jesus was a prophet not a scribe. A. W. Tozer notes the difference between a prophet and a scribe, "for the scribe tells us what he has read, and the prophet tells what he has seen."[49] Luke presented Jesus as a prophet like the Old Testament prophets whose words were inspired by the Spirit. The word of Jesus was effective to bring about change. The word of Jesus was also a powerful word of command. O'Reilly asserts that the word of Jesus, which consists of powerful preaching, and the word that effectively casts out demons and heals the sick

---

49. Tozer, *Pursuit of God*, 49. Tozer believed that the distinction is not an imaginary one. Between the scribe who has read and the prophet who has seen there is a difference as wide as the sea. We are overrun today with orthodox scribes, but the prophets, where are they? The hard voice of the scribe sounds over evangelicalism, but the church waits for the tender voice of the saint who has penetrated the veil and has gazed with the inward eye upon the wonder that is God. Tozer, 49. Similarly, Hawthorne asserts that the Spirit illumined Jesus's mind, gave him insight into the truth of God, and enabled him to speak with an authoritatively convicting power never experienced by the scribes, the learned teachers of the Jewish law, or by the Pharisees, the guardians of the Law. See Hawthorne, *Presence and the Power*, 231.

are both powerful in exactly the same way because the power in each case derives from the same source, viz. the power of the Spirit that Jesus received at his baptism.[50] This complementary view was demonstrated in this work.

First, in the testimony of Jesus (chapter 2), which was the Nazareth manifesto, the complementary view of words and works was argued. In Nazareth, the people were startled at Jesus's words of grace. The words of grace were the divine influence present in the words that gave the words their tangible impact. Luke described the manner of the sermon as riveting from the beginning to the end. He also described the manner or attitude of the people during the sermon. The response of the people was at first favorable, but then there was a shift in mood. They became skeptical and chose to harbor unbelief in their hearts, which led to their rejection of him. For Luke, the words of Jesus were profound and worked mightily by calling for immediate decision from the people. Unfortunately, those in Nazareth chose to reject the gracious words, which led to their doom, while those in Capernaum accepted his words and were blessed by his ministry (Luke 4:28–44). Forbes says, "Preaching under the anointing of the Spirit deeply touches the hearer, evoking either acceptance or rejection of the gospel."[51]

Second, the testimony of the two disciples walking to Emmaus (chapter 3), presents a complementary view of words and works. The description of Jesus as a prophet mighty in words and mighty in works was from the testimony of the two disciples. After the two had given their verdict of the life and ministry of Jesus to a stranger walking with them. The stranger, who happens to be the resurrected Jesus, rebukes their skepticism and doubt about the resurrection. Luke stated that Jesus then began an exposition of himself from Moses and from all the prophets to his doubting disciples, after which the two disciples would later say, "Were not our hearts burning within us as he spoke to us on the road, as he opened the Scripture?" Indeed, his words were burning and powerful that they resulted (worked) in conviction and change of mind and heart in the two disciples.

Finally, in the speech of Peter at the house of Cornelius (chapter 5), Peter affirmed the complementary view. Peter began his speech by affirming the preaching ministry of Jesus, he says, "As to the word that he sent to the

---

50. O'Reilly, *Word and Sign*, 38.
51. Forbes, *Holy Spirit & Preaching*, 42.

children of Israel, proclaiming peace through Jesus, who is Lord of all." Next, he went on to affirm the works of Jesus by asserting that Jesus went about doing good and healing all who were oppressed by the devil. According to Peter, Jesus's words of peace and work of peace in the lives of the people were possible because the Spirit anointed him. Undoubtedly, the same Spirit that empowered Jesus and the apostles lives today in every Christian. Shelton notes that "believers have received from Jesus the same Holy Spirit that empowered him, and Luke expects that the Spirit-words and Spirit-works will continue in the church."[52]

## A Witness Mighty in Words and Works Today

God is still calling preachers today to be channels through which the Holy Spirit's power will be manifested to the world through mighty words and works. Jowett says, "Our mission is to be one of emancipation both by word and work, by gospel and by crusade."[53] Jesus announced to his disciples and those who would later believe in him a great promise. He says, "Truly, truly, I say to you, he who believes in me, the works that I do, he will do also; and greater works than these he will do; because I go to the Father" (John 14:12). The greater works Jesus was referring to in this verse are the advancement of the gospel through mighty words and works especially in conversion.[54] Jesus promised believers to do greater works than him because he is going back to the Father. By going back to the Father his redemptive work was approved, and therefore the Holy Spirit was poured out to all believers (Acts 2:33). The evidence of the Spirit's empowerment is seen in the preacher's life and in the hearers.

First, the empowerment of the Spirit is present in the life and words of the preacher. There is an atmosphere of life around the preacher brought about

---

52. Shelton, *Mighty in Word*, 81.

53. Jowett, *Preacher*, 34.

54. This is obvious from the records of conversion that Luke noted in Acts of the Apostles. On the day of Pentecost, three thousand souls were converted (Acts 2:41); in chapter 4 of Acts about five thousand (4:4); in chapter 5 multitudes (5:14); and many more passages (6:7; 9:31; 9:35; 9:42; 11:21; 11:24; 12:24; 13:48–49; 16:5; 17:4; 17:11–12; 18:8; 19:20). This is not to say that mighty words and works will always be positive because Luke also recorded the many rejections and persecution experienced by the apostles (Acts 5:17–42; 6:12; 8:1–3; 9:1–2; 12:1–19; 13:50–51; 14:19; 16:19–24; 17:5–9; 18:6; 19:23–41; 21:30–32).

by his spirituality, which is active in silence as well as in speech.[55] There is wholeness in the character of the preacher, which surrenders to divine guidance and direction (Acts 8:29; 10:19–20; 16:6–10). The preacher is also full of wisdom and knowledge (Acts 6:10). Holden says, "It is one thing to be born of the Spirit, and another to be filled with Him in such way as that He controls and guides and sanctifies the whole life, which becomes in truth a 'temple of the Holy Spirit.'"[56] Apart from the character of the preacher, the speech of the preacher is transformed as well. There is boldness and courage in speech (Acts 4:13, 31); there is an effective utterance (Acts 2:4; 6:9–10), which gives the speech force and persuasion. All of these happen to the preacher because of the empowerment of the Spirit upon him. In sum, Bounds says, "It is this unction which gives the words of the preacher such point, sharpness, and power, and which creates such friction and stir in many a dead congregation."[57] He also describes the empowerment in the life of the preacher in a profound way. He noted that it is the unction that inspires and clarifies the preacher's intellect, and gives insight and projecting power. It gives to the preacher heart power, which is greater than head power, and tenderness, purity, force flow from the heart by it. Enlargement, freedom, fullness of thought, directness, and simplicity of utterance are the fruits of this unction.[58]

Second, the empowerment of the Spirit is also visible in its working in the hearers. Vines and Shaddix describe the impact of the anointing (empowerment) on both preacher and hearers. They write,

---

55. Jowett, *Preacher*, 59. Conversely, Jowett also described the consequences of working without the power of the Spirit. He asserts, "We shall lack that fine fragrance which makes people know that we dwell in 'the king's garden.' There will be no 'heavenly air' about our spirits. Atmospheres will not be mysteriously changed by our presence. We shall no longer bring the strength of mountain-air into close and fusty fellowships." Furthermore, he states,

> Our speech lacks a mysterious impressiveness. We are wordy but we are not mighty. We are eloquent but we do not persuade. We are reasonable but we do not woo. We make a "show of power" but men do not move. Men come and go, they may be interested or amused, but they do not bow in penitent surrender at the feet of the Lord. We go on talking, talking, talking, and the haunts of "the evil one" ring with scorn of our futility. Our words are just the "enticing words of man's wisdom," they are not "in demonstration of the Spirit and of power."

Jowett, 58–60.

56. Holden, *Price of Power*, 26.
57. Bounds, *Power Through Prayer*, 89.
58. Bounds, 90.

> The anointing keeps the preacher aware of a power not his own. In the best sense of the word, he is "possessed" – caught up in the message by the power of the Spirit. He becomes a channel used by the Holy Spirit. At the same time the people are gripped, moved, convicted. When the Holy Spirit takes over in the preaching event, something miraculous happens.[59]

The effective word of a Spirit-empowered preacher will either result in transformation or condemnation as seen in the ministry of Jesus and the apostles. This is because the preacher's word is empowered by the Spirit, and the word of God (Scripture) is living and active (Heb 4:12). When it is accepted, it brings the divine life to a person. A life manifested in healing, restoration, sharing, loving, binding up the broken hearted, giving hope to the downtrodden, serving, and filling the earth with the glory of the Lord in the person of Christ who is the focus of preaching. On the other hand, when it is rejected, it becomes a word of judgment and eternal condemnation. It should be noted also that rejection is not due to the weakness of the word; Luke attributes it to the devil or the dispositions of the hearers.[60] Furthermore, the goal of the word is not to condemn but to unite people to Christ and his body (church). However, in order to unite those who believe in Jesus and accept his word, the word must first separate those who are willing to believe from those who are not.[61]

---

59. Vines and Shaddix, *Power in the Pulpit*, 66.

60. O'Reilly, *Word and Sign*, 109. According to O'Reilly, the failure of some to accept the word and repent is not to be attributed to any deficiency in the word itself. The parable of the sower, and particularly the Lucan interpretation of that parable, makes it clear that if the word does not take root and flourish, the failure is to be attributed to the devil or the dispositions of the hearer. The reason why "those along the path" in the parable are not converted is that "the devil comes and takes away the word from their hearts, that they may not believe and be saved" (8:12). In the case of "what fell among thorns" (v. 14), Luke's interpretation of the parable differs significantly from the parallels. In Matthew and Mark the word cannot bear fruit in these circumstances because it is choked by the thorns, but in Luke it is not the word but the hearers who are choked. The word is too powerful to be overcome by such obstacles. What really matters where the word is concerned are the dispositions of the heart. It is not enough simply to hear the word with the ears, one must hold on to them with "an honest and good heart" (v. 15) if it is to bear fruit. In one of the short sayings that follow the interpretation of the parable we find once more that Luke differs significantly from what would appear to be his source: Mark's saying runs, "Take heed what you hear" (4:24), whereas Luke's is, "Take heed how you hear" (v. 18). He is at pains to emphasize the importance of hearing the word properly. O'Reilly, *Word and Sign*.

61. O'Reilly, 76. O'Reilly analyzed the preaching of Peter on the day of Pentecost and came to a conclusion that is significant to note in this work. He holds that the effects of the word bear witness to its power and to the Spirit who inspires it. It is a living, active word, which

In sum, a witness cannot tell of emancipation unless they have encountered it. Long says, "We can give testimony only about that which we have experienced. This does not imply that we have to understand everything before we can bear witness."[62] The preacher has been sent to the Scriptures by the Spirit, they are guided through careful exegesis of the biblical text, they perceive through the Spirit the authorial intent of the text, which they then go to proclaim passionately and powerfully to the people. Long says, "The move from text to sermon is a move from beholding to attesting, from seeing to saying, from listening to telling, from perceiving to testifying, from being a witness to bearing witness."[63] Thus, the Holy Spirit manifest in the life of the witness, the preparation of their sermon, the delivery of the sermon, and the Spirit also impacts the receptivity of the hearers. When this manifestation happens in preaching, one can say emphatically, "God has visited his people in the person and work of Christ." This is exactly what happened in the witness of the apostles and other witnesses in Acts. Hawthorne believes that the Acts of the Apostles was intended to show something of the nature of those things that God is able to do through people who yield themselves willingly to the influence of the Spirit.[64]

---

can penetrate to the depths of the person who hears it and effect a radical change in him. It brings about a division between those who accept it and those who do not, for in the face of this address no one can remain neutral. The word molds those who accept it into a new community around the risen Lord. It also causes that community to grow in numbers and extent beyond all human expectations and that in spite of opposition and persecution. It sustains the life of the community it has created and builds it up interiorly. It deepens the faith and love of those who belong to the community and by so doing gives the missionary endeavor fresh inspiration and power. Finally, the word confers salvation on those who believe. This salvation consists in forgiveness of sins, fellowship with other believers in the community, and fellowship with Jesus, the risen Lord. See O'Reilly, 90.

62. Long, *Witness of Preaching*, 99.
63. Long, 100.
64. Hawthorne, *Presence and the Power*, 238. Hawthorne goes on to say,

> Through the Spirit those people of the very early church were enabled to preach boldly, convincingly, and authoritatively (Acts 2:14–41), to face crises and surmount obstacles with a courage and resoluteness and power they never dreamed they had (4:29–31), to cheerfully face persecution and suffering, and even to accept death with a prayer of forgiveness (5:40–41; 7:55–60), to heal the sick and raise the dead (9:36–41; 28:8), to arbitrate differences and bring about peace (15:1–35), to know where to go and where not to go, what to do and what not to do (16:6–10; 21:10–11), and so on."

See Hawthorne, 238.

# Bibliography

Akin, Daniel L., David Lewis Allen, and Ned Lee Mathews. *Text-Driven Preaching: God's Word at the Heart of Every Sermon*. Nashville: B&H Academic, 2010.

Allen, David L. *The Extent of the Atonement: A Historical and Critical Review*. Nashville: B&H Academic, 2016.

Allen, Ronald J. *Preaching Luke-Acts*. St. Louis: Chalice Press, 2000.

Aristotle. *The Rhetoric of Aristotle: An Expanded Translation with Supplementary Examples for Students of Composition and Public Speaking*. Translated by Lane Cooper. New Jersey: Prentice-Hall, 1932.

Arrington, Yancey. *Tap: Defeating the Sins That Defeat You*. League City, TX: Clear Creek Resources, 2010.

Arthurs, Jeffrey D. *Preaching with Variety: How to Re-create the Dynamics of Biblical Genres*. Grand Rapids: Kregel Academic, 2007.

Atkinson, William. *Baptism in the Spirit: Luke-Acts and the Dunn Debate*. Eugene, OR: Pickwick, 2011.

Azurdia III, Arturo G. *Spirit Empowered Preaching: Involving the Holy Spirit in Your Ministry*. Fearn, England: Christian Focus Publication, 1998.

Barrett, C. K. *A Critical and Exegetical Commentary on the Acts of the Apostles*. Vol. 1. Edinburgh: T&T Clark, 1994.

Bauer, Walter. *A Greek-English Lexicon of the New Testament* [BDAG]. Edited and translated by William F. Arndt, F. Wilber Gingrich, and Frederick W. Danker. 3rd ed. Chicago: University of Chicago Press, 2000.

Beach, Mark J. "The Kingdom of God: A Brief Exposition of its Meaning and Implications." *Mid-America Journal of Theology* 23 (2012): 53–76.

Bickel, Bruce R. *Light and Heat: The Puritan View of the Pulpit*. Morgan, PA: Soli Deo Gloria Publications, 1999.

Bisagno, John R. *Letters to Timothy: A Handbook for Pastors*. Nashville: B&H Publishing, 2001.

Blomberg, Craig L. *Jesus and the Gospels: An Introduction and Survey*. 2nd ed. Nashville: B&H Publishing, 2009.

Bock, Darrell L. *Acts*. Baker Exegetical Commentary on the New Testament. Grand Rapids: Baker Academic, 2007.

———. *Luke 1:1–9:50*. Vol. 1. Baker Exegetical Commentary on the New Testament. Grand Rapids: Baker Academic, 1994.

———. *Luke 9:51–24:53*. Vol. 2. Baker Exegetical Commentary on the New Testament. Grand Rapids: Baker Academic, 1996.

———. *Luke*. The IVP New Testament Commentary Series. Downers Grove: InterVarsity Press, 1994.

———. *A Theology of Luke and Acts: Biblical Theology of the New Testament*. Edited by Andreas J. Köstenberger. Grand Rapids: Zondervan, 2012.

Bolt, Peter G. "Mission and Witness." In *Witness to the Gospel: The Theology of Acts*, edited by I. Howard Marshall and David Peterson, 191–214. Grand Rapids: Eerdmans, 1998.

Bonhoeffer, Dietrich. *Worldly Preaching: Lectures on Homiletics*. Edited by Clyde E. Fant. New York: Crossroad, 1975.

Bounds, E. M. *Power Through Prayer*. Chicago: Moody, 2009.

Bridges, Charles. *The Christian Ministry with an Inquiry into the Causes of Its Inefficiency*. East Peoria: Versa Press, 2009.

Brooks, James A., and Carlton L. Winbery. *Syntax of New Testament Greek*. Lanham, MD: University Press of America, 1979.

Brooks, Phillips. *The Joy of Preaching*. Grand Rapids: Kregel, 1989.

Brown, Henry Clifton. *Steps to the Sermon: A Plan for Sermon Preparation*. Nashville: Broadman Press, 1963.

Browne, R. E. C. *The Ministry of the Word*. Philadelphia: Fortress, 1976.

Bruce, F. F. *The Acts of the Apostles: The Greek Text with Introduction and Commentary*. Rev. ed. Grand Rapids: Eerdmans, 1990.

———. *The Speeches in the Acts of the Apostles*. London: Tyndale Press, 1943.

Brueggemann, Walter. *Cadences of Home: Preaching Among Exiles*. Louisville: Westminster John Knox, 1997.

———. *Finally Comes the Poet: Daring Speech for Proclamation*. Minneapolis: Fortress, 1989.

Bullinger, E. W. *Figures of Speech Used in the Bible: Explained and Illustrated*. Grand Rapids: Baker Books, 1999.

Bultmann, Rudolf. "The Concept of the Word of God in the New Testament." In *Faith and Understanding*, vol. 1, edited by Robert W. Funk, translated by Louise Pettibone Smith, 286–312. New York: Harper & Row, 1966.

Buttrick, David. *A Captive Voice: The Liberation of Preaching*. Louisville: Westminster John Knox, 1994.

Carson, D. A., and Douglas J. Moo. *An Introduction to the New Testament*. 2nd ed. Grand Rapids: Zondervan, 1992.

Clark, Andrew C. "The Role of the Apostles." In *Witness to the Gospel: The Theology of Acts*, edited by I. Howard Marshall and David Peterson, 177–90. Grand Rapids: Eerdmans, 1998.

Conzelmann, Hans. *Act of the Apostles: A Commentary on the Acts of the Apostles*. Philadelphia: Fortress, 1987.

Cox, James W. *Preaching: A Comprehensive Approach to the Design and Delivery of Sermons*. San Francisco: Harper & Row, 1985.

Craddock, Fred B. *Preaching*. Nashville: Abingdon, 1985.

———. *As One without Authority*. Rev. ed., with New Sermons. St. Louis: Chalice Press, 2001.

Cranfield, Charles E. B. *A Critical and Exegetical Commentary on the Epistle to the Romans*. Vol. 1. Edinburgh: T&T Clark, 2001.

Crockett, Larrimore C. "Luke 4:25–27 and Jewish-Gentile Relations in Luke-Acts." *Journal of Biblical Literature* 88, no. 2 (1969): 177–83.

Culy, Martin M., Mikeal C. Parsons, and Joshua J. Stigall. *Acts: A Handbook on the Greek Text*. Waco, TX: Baylor University Press, 2003.

———. *Luke: A Handbook on the Greek Text*. Waco, TX: Baylor University Press, 2010.

Custer, Stewart. *Witness to Christ: A Commentary on Acts*. Greenville, SC: Bob Jones University Press, 2000.

Danker, Frederick W. *Luke*. Proclamation Commentaries. Edited by Gerhard Krode. Philadelphia: Fortress, 1975.

Davis, H. Grady. *Design for Preaching*. Philadelphia: Fortress, 1958.

Dibelius, Martin. *A Fresh Approach to the New Testament and Early Christian Literature*. New York: Scribner's Sons, 1936.

Dillon, Richard J. *From Eye-Witnesses to Ministers of the Word: Tradition and Composition in Luke 24*. Rome: Biblical Institute Press, 1978.

Dodd, C. H. *The Apostolic Preaching and its Development*. New York: Harper & Brothers, 1962.

Dunn, James D. G. *Baptism in the Holy Spirit: A Re-examination of the New Testament Teaching on the Gift of the Spirit in Relation to Pentecostalism Today*. Naperville: Alec R. Allenson, 1970.

———. *Romans 1–8*. Word Biblical Commentary 38A. Dallas: Word Books, 1988.

Ellis, Earle E. *The Gospel of Luke*. The New Century Bible Commentary. Grand Rapids: Eerdmans, 1996.

Evans, Craig A., and James Sanders. *Luke and Scripture: The Function of Sacred Tradition in Luke-Acts*. Minneapolis: Fortress, 1993.

Falcetta, Alessandro. *The Call of Nazareth: Form and Exegesis of Luke 4:16–30*. Paris: Gabalda, 2003.

Fanning, Buist M. *Verbal Aspect in New Testament Greek*. Oxford: Clarendon, 1990.

Fee, Gordon D. *New Testament Exegesis: A Handbook for Students and Pastors*. 3rd ed. Louisville: Westminster John Knox, 2002.
Fitzmyer, Joseph. *The Acts of the Apostles: A New Translation with Introduction and Commentary*. New York: Doubleday, 1998.
———. *The Gospel According to Luke I–IX*. Vol. 28. New York: Doubleday, 1981.
———. *The Gospel According to Luke X–XXIV*. Vol. 28. New York: Doubleday, 1985.
Forbes, James. *The Holy Spirit & Preaching*. Nashville: Abingdon Press, 1989.
France, R. T. *Jesus and the Old Testament: His Application of Old Testament Passages to Himself and His Mission*. London: Tyndale Press, 1971.
Friedrich, Gerhard, ed. *Theological Dictionary of the New Testament*. Vol. 9. Grand Rapids: Eerdmans, 1968.
Garland, David E. *Luke*. Zondervan Exegetical Commentary on the New Testament, vol. 3. Grand Rapids: Zondervan, 2011.
Geisler, Norman L. *Chosen but Free: A Balanced View of God's Sovereignty and Free Will*. 3rd ed. Minneapolis: Bethany House, 2010.
Gempf, Conrad. "Public Speaking and Published Accounts." In *The Book of Acts in Its First Century Setting*, vol. 1, edited by Bruce W. Winter and Andrew D. Clarke, 259–303. Grand Rapids: Eerdmans, 1993.
Ger, Steven. *The Book of Acts: Witnesses to the World*. Twenty-First Century Biblical Commentary Series. Chattanooga, TN: AMG Publishers, 2004.
Godet, Frederic Louis. *Commentary on Luke*. Grand Rapids: Kregel, 1981.
Green, Joel B. *The Gospel of Luke*. The New International Commentary on the New Testament. Grand Rapids: Eerdmans, 1997.
———. *The Theology of the Gospel of Luke*. Cambridge: Cambridge University Press, 1995.
Green, Michael. *I Believe in the Holy Spirit*. Rev. ed. Grand Rapids: Eerdmans, 2004.
Haenchen, Ernst. *The Acts of the Apostles*. Oxford: Blackwell, 1971.
Hastings, Adrian. *Prophet and Witness in Jerusalem: A Study of the Teaching of Saint Luke*. Baltimore, MD: Helicon, 1958.
Hawthorne, Gerald F. *The Presence and the Power: The Significance of the Holy Spirit in the Life and Ministry of Jesus*. Eugene, OR: Wipf and Stock, 1991.
Heisler, Greg. *Spirit-Led Preaching: The Holy Spirit's Role in Sermon Preparation and Delivery*. Nashville: B&H Academic, 2007.
Hirsch, Jr., E. D. *Validity in Interpretation*. London: Yale University Press, 1967.
Holden, Stuart J. *The Price of Power*. New York: Marshall Brothers, 1918.
Hull, J. H. E. *The Holy Spirit in the Acts of the Apostles*. New York: World Publishing, 1968.
Hur, Ju. *A Dynamic Reading of the Holy Spirit in Luke-Acts*. Sheffield: Sheffield Academic Press, 2001.

Ignace De La Potterie, S. J. "The Anointing of Christ." In *Word and Mystery: Biblical Essays on the Person and Mission of Christ*, edited by Leo J. O'Donovan, 155–84. New York: Newman Press, 1968.
Iorg, Jeff. *Is God Calling Me?: Answering the Question Every Believer Asks*. Nashville: B&H Publishing, 2008.
Johns, Cheryl Bridges. "Holy Spirit and Preaching." In *The New Interpreter's Handbook of Preaching*, edited by Wilson, Paul Scott, 460–61. Nashville: Abingdon, 2008.
Jowett, J. H. *The Preacher: His Life and Work*. Grand Rapids: Baker Books, 1968.
Keddie, Gordon J. *You Are My Witnesses: The Message of the Acts of the Apostles*. Darlington: Evangelical Press, 2000.
Keener, S. Craig. *Acts: Introduction and 1:1–2:47*. Vol. 1. An Exegetical Commentary. Grand Rapids: Baker Academic, 2012.
———. *Acts: 3:1–14:28*. Vol. 2. An Exegetical Commentary. Grand Rapids: Baker Academic, 2013.
Krodel, Gerhard. *Acts*. Proclamation Commentaries. Philadelphia: Fortress, 1981.
Kuruvilla, Abraham. *Privilege the Text!: A Theological Hermeneutic for Preaching*. Chicago: Moody, 2013.
Ladd, George Eldon. *A Theology of the New Testament*. Rev. ed. Edited by Donald A. Hagner. Grand Rapids: Eerdmans, 1974.
Larkin, Jr., William J. *Acts*. IVP New Testament Commentary Series. Downers Grove: InterVarsity Press, 1995.
Lenski, R. C. H. *The Interpretation of the Acts of the Apostles*. Minneapolis: Augsburg, 1961.
Liefield, Walter L. *Interpreting the Book of Acts*. Guide to New Testament Exegesis. Grand Rapids: Baker Books, 1995.
———. *New Testament Exposition: From Text to Sermon*. Grand Rapids: Zondervan, 1984.
Lischer, Richard. *A Theology of Preaching: The Dynamics of the Gospel*. Rev. ed. Eugene, OR: Wipf & Stock, 1992.
Lloyd-Jones, Martyn D. *Preaching and Preachers*. Grand Rapids: Zondervan, 1971.
Long, Thomas G. *The Witness of Preaching*. 2nd ed. Louisville: Westminster John Knox, 2005.
———. *Preaching and the Literary Forms of the Bible*. Philadelphia: Fortress, 1985.
Lotz, Denton. "Peter's Wider Understanding of God's Will: Acts 10:34–48." *International Reviews on Mission* 77, no. 306 (1988): 201–7.
Lowry, Eugene L. *The Homiletical Plot: The Sermon as Narrative Art Form*. Louisville: Westminster John Knox, 2001.
Maddox, Robert. *The Purpose of Luke-Acts*. Edited by John Riches. Edinburgh: T&T Clark, 1982.

Marshall, I. H. *The Acts of the Apostles*. New Testament Guides. Sheffield: Sheffield Academic Press Ltd, 2001.

———. *Luke: Historian and Theologian*. Grand Rapids: Zondervan, 1989.

———. *The Gospel of Luke*. The New International Greek Testament Commentary. Exeter: Paternoster, 1978.

Martin, Robert J. *All About Witnessing: A Study of the Book of Acts*. Grand Rapids: Baker Books, 1975.

Menzies, Robert P. *The Development of Early Christian Pneumatology: With Special Reference to Luke-Acts*. Sheffield: Sheffield Academic Press, 1991.

———. *Empowered for Witness: The Spirit in Luke-Acts*. Sheffield: Sheffield Academic Press, 1991.

Metzger, Bruce M. *A Textual Commentary on the Greek New Testament*. 2nd ed. New York: United Bible Societies, 2012.

Mitchell, Alan C. "A Prophet Mighty in Deed and Word: Luke's Presentation of Jesus as the Messiah." *The Bible Today* 48 (June, 2010): 329–34.

Moo, Douglas J. *The Epistle to the Romans*. New International Commentary on the New Testament. Grand Rapids: Eerdmans, 1996.

Morris, Leon. *The Epistle to the Romans*. Grand Rapids: Eerdmans, 1988.

Moule, C. F. D. *Christ's Messengers: Studies in the Acts of the Apostles*. New York: Association Press, 1957.

Moulton, James Hope. *A Grammar of New Testament Greek*. Vol. 3. Edinburgh: T&T Clark, 1963.

Mounce, Robert H. *Romans*. The New American Commentary, vol. 27. Nashville: Broadman & Holman, 1995.

Nolland, John. *Luke 1–9:20*. Word Biblical Commentary 35A. Waco, TX: Word Books, Publisher, 1989.

———. "Words of Grace (Luke 4,22)." *Biblica* 65, no. 1 (1984): 44–60.

Olford, Stephen F., and David L. Olford. *Anointed Expository Preaching*. Nashville: B&H Academic, 1998.

O'Neill, J. C. *The Theology of Acts in Its Historical Setting*. Rev. ed. London: SPCK, 1970.

———. *Paul's Letter to the Romans*. Harmondsworth: Penguin Books, 1975.

O'Reilly, Leo. *Word and Sign in the Acts of the Apostles: A Study in Lucan Theology*. Roma: Editrice Pontificia Universita Gregoriana, 1987.

Osborne, Grant R. *The Hermeneutical Spiral: A Comprehensive Introduction to Biblical Interpretation*. Revised edition. Downers Grove: InterVarsity Press, 2006.

O'Toole, Robert F. "Εἰρήνην, an Underlying Theme in Acts 10:34–43." *Biblica* 77, no. 4 (1996): 461–76.

Owen, John. *Overcoming Sin and Temptation*. Edited by Kelly M. Kapic and Justin Taylor. Wheaton, IL: Crossway, 2006.

Packer, J. I. *God Has Spoken: Revelation and the Bible*. 3rd ed. Grand Rapids: Baker Books, 1993.

Padilla, Osvaldo. *The Acts of the Apostles: Interpretation, History and Theology*. Downers Grove: InterVarsity Press, 2016.

Pervo, Richard I. *Acts*. Edited by Harold W. Attridge. Minneapolis: Fortress Press, 2009.

———. *Dating Acts: Between the Evangelists and the Apologists*. Santa Rosa, CA: Polebridge Press, 2006.

Piper, John. *The Supremacy of God in Preaching*. Rev. ed. Grand Rapids: Baker Books. 2004.

Polhill, John B. *Acts*. The New American Commentary 26. Nashville: Broadman Press, 1992.

Porter, Stanley E. *Idioms of the Greek New Testament: Biblical Languages Greek*. Sheffield: Sheffield Academic Press, 1992.

Powell, Mark Allan. *What Are They Saying About Acts?* New York: Paulist Press, 1991.

Prime, Derek, and Alistair Begg. *On Being a Pastor: Understanding Our Calling and Work*. Chicago: Moody, 2004.

Ramm, Bernard L. *The Witness of the Spirit: An Essay on the Contemporary Relevance of the Internal Witness of the Holy Spirit*. Grand Rapids: Eerdmans, 1959.

Ricoeur, Paul. "The Hermeneutics of Testimony." In *Essays on Biblical Interpretation*, edited by Lewis Seymour Mudge, 119–49. Philadelphia: Fortress, 1980.

Robertson, A. T. *A Grammar of the Greek New Testament in the Light of Historical Research*. Nashville: Broadman Press, 1934.

———. *Word Pictures in the New Testament*. Concise ed. Edited by James A. Swanson. Nashville: Broadman Press, 2000.

Schweizer, Eduard. *The Good News According to Luke*. Translated by David E. Green. Atlanta: John Knox, 1984.

Shelton, James B. *Mighty in Word and Deed: The Role of the Holy Spirit in Luke-Acts*. Peabody: Hendrickson, 1991.

Sloan, Robert Bryan. *The Favorable Year of the Lord: A Study of Jubilary Theology in the Gospel of Luke*. Austin, TX: Schola Press, 1977.

Smith, Steven W. *Recapturing the Voice of God: Shaping Sermons Like Scripture*. Nashville: B&H Academic, 2015.

Soards, Marion L. *The Speeches in Acts: Their Content, Context, and Concerns*. Louisville: John Knox, 1994.

Sproul, R. C. *Chosen by God*. Wheaton: Tyndale House, 1995.

Spurgeon, Charles H. *Lectures to My Students*. Peabody, MA: Hendrickson, 2012.

Stein, Robert H. *Luke*. The New American Commentary 24. Nashville: Broadman Press, 1992.

Stott, John R. W. *Baptism & Fullness: The Work of the Holy Spirit Today*. Downers Grove: InterVarsity Press, 1976.

———. *Between Two Worlds: The Challenge of Preaching Today*. Grand Rapids: Eerdmans, 1984.

———. *The Preacher's Portrait*. Grand Rapids: Eerdmans, 1961.

Streett, Alan R. "The Public Invitation and Calvinism." In *Whosoever Will: A Biblical-Theological Critique of Five-Point Calvinism*, edited by David L. Allen and Steve Lemke, 233–52. Nashville: B&H Publishing, 2010.

Summers, Ray. *Commentary on Luke: Jesus, the Universal Savior*. Waco, TX: Word Books, 1972.

Talbert, Charles H. "The Lukan Presentation of Jesus' Ministry in Galilee." *Review & Expositor* 64, no. 4 (1967): 485–97.

———. *Reading Acts: A Literary and Theological Commentary on the Acts of the Apostles*. New York: Crossroad, 1997.

———. *Reading Acts: A Literary and Theological Commentary on the Acts of the Apostles*. Rev. ed. Macon: Smyth & Helwys, 2005.

———. *Reading Luke: A Literary and Theological Commentary on the Third Gospel*. New York: Crossroad, 1984.

Tannehill, Robert C. *Luke*. Abingdon New Testament Commentaries. Nashville: Abingdon Press, 1996.

———. *The Narrative Unity of Luke–Acts: A Literary Interpretation*. Vol. 1. Philadelphia: Fortress, 1986.

Tenery Robert M., and J. Steve Sells. *With Greater Power: The Secret to a Spirit-Empowered Life*. Self-published, 2010.

Thiselton, Anthony C. *New Horizons in Hermeneutics: The Theory and Practice of Transforming Biblical Reading*. Grand Rapids: Zondervan, 1992.

Thucydides, and Richard Crawley. *The History of the Peloponnesian War*. New Zealand, Auckland: Floating Press, 2008. *EBSCOhost*.

Tiede David L. *Luke*. Augsburg Commentary on the New Testament. Minneapolis: Augsburg, 1988.

Tozer, A. W. *The Pursuit of God*. Chicago: Moody, 2006.

Turner, Max. "Luke and the Spirit: Renewing Theological Interpretation of Biblical Pneumatology." In *Reading Luke: Interpretation, Reflection, Formation*, edited by Craig G. Bartholomew, Joel B. Green, and Anthony C. Thiselton, 267–93. Grand Rapids: Zondervan, 2005.

Vanhoozer, Kevin J. *Is there a Meaning in this Text?: The Bible, the Reader, and the Morality of Literary Knowledge*. Grand Rapids: Zondervan, 1998.

Vines, Jerry, and Jim Shaddix. *Power in the Pulpit: How to Prepare and Deliver Expository Sermons*. Chicago: Moody, 1999.

Vlach, Michael J. "The Kingdom of God in Paul's Epistles." *The Master's Seminary Journal* 26, no. 1 (Spring 2015): 59–74.

Wallace, Daniel B. *Greek Grammar Beyond the Basics: An Exegetical Syntax of the New Testament*. Grand Rapids: Zondervan, 1996.

Weatherspoon, Jesse. B. *Sent Forth to Preach: Studies in Apostolic Preaching*. New York: Harper & Brothers, 1954.

Wegner, Paul D. *A Student's Guide to Textual Criticism of the Bible: Its History, Methods and Results*. Downer Grove: InterVarsity Press, 2006.

Whitney, Donald S. *Spiritual Disciplines for the Christian Life*. Colorado Springs: Navpress, 1991.

Willimon, William H. "Overcoming Pentecost in Our Preaching: Proclamation Without Spirit." *Journal for Preachers* 24, no. 4 (2001): 31–34.

Wolfe, Kenneth R. "The Chiastic Structure of Luke-Acts and Some Implications for Worship." *Southwestern Journal of Theology* 22, no. 2 (1980): 60–71.

Zerwick, Maximilian. *Biblical Greek: Illustrated by Examples*. Rome: Scripta Pontificii Instituti Biblici, 1963.

Langham Literature, with its publishing work, is a ministry of Langham Partnership.

Langham Partnership is a global fellowship working in pursuit of the vision God entrusted to its founder John Stott –

> *to facilitate the growth of the church in maturity and Christ-likeness through raising the standards of biblical preaching and teaching.*

**Our vision** is to see churches in the Majority World equipped for mission and growing to maturity in Christ through the ministry of pastors and leaders who believe, teach and live by the word of God.

**Our mission** is to strengthen the ministry of the word of God through:
- nurturing national movements for biblical preaching
- fostering the creation and distribution of evangelical literature
- enhancing evangelical theological education

especially in countries where churches are under-resourced.

**Our ministry**

*Langham Preaching* partners with national leaders to nurture indigenous biblical preaching movements for pastors and lay preachers all around the world. With the support of a team of trainers from many countries, a multi-level programme of seminars provides practical training, and is followed by a programme for training local facilitators. Local preachers' groups and national and regional networks ensure continuity and ongoing development, seeking to build vigorous movements committed to Bible exposition.

*Langham Literature* provides Majority World preachers, scholars and seminary libraries with evangelical books and electronic resources through publishing and distribution, grants and discounts. The programme also fosters the creation of indigenous evangelical books in many languages, through writer's grants, strengthening local evangelical publishing houses, and investment in major regional literature projects, such as one volume Bible commentaries like the *Africa Bible Commentary* and the *South Asia Bible Commentary*.

*Langham Scholars* provides financial support for evangelical doctoral students from the Majority World so that, when they return home, they may train pastors and other Christian leaders with sound, biblical and theological teaching. This programme equips those who equip others. Langham Scholars also works in partnership with Majority World seminaries in strengthening evangelical theological education. A growing number of Langham Scholars study in high quality doctoral programmes in the Majority World itself. As well as teaching the next generation of pastors, graduated Langham Scholars exercise significant influence through their writing and leadership.

To learn more about Langham Partnership and the work we do visit **langham.org**

www.ingramcontent.com/pod-product-compliance
Lightning Source LLC
Chambersburg PA
CBHW070614170426
43200CB00012B/2690